The
School-Home
Connection

*This book is dedicated to my father, August Scalero, who taught
me to learn from my mistakes, strive to improve my successes, and never give
less than 110 percent effort into whatever I chose to do. This book is also dedicated
to my mother, Elenia, who showed me, on a regular basis, that good relationships
are essential to our success and happiness.*

—Rosemary Olender

The
School-Home
Connection

Forging Positive
Relationships
With Parents

Rosemary A. Olender
Jacquelyn Elias
Rosemary D. Mastroleo

CORWIN
A SAGE Company

For information:

Corwin
A SAGE Company
2455 Teller Road
Thousand Oaks, California 91320
(800) 233-9936
Fax: (800) 417-2466
www.corwin.com

SAGE India Pvt. Ltd.
B 1/I 1 Mohan Cooperative
    Industrial Area
Mathura Road, New Delhi 110 044
India

SAGE Ltd.
1 Oliver's Yard
55 City Road
London EC1Y 1SP
United Kingdom

SAGE Asia-Pacific Pte. Ltd.
33 Pekin Street #02-01
Far East Square
Singapore 048763

Printed in the United States of America

Library of Congress Cataloging-in-Publication Data

Olender, Rosemary A.
The school-home connection: forging positive relationships with parents/Rosemary A. Olender, Jacquelyn Elias, Rosemary D. Mastroleo.
        p. cm.
Includes bibliographical references and index.
ISBN 978-1-4129-6864-5 (pbk.)
    1. Parent-teacher relationships. 2. Teacher-student relationships. 3. Education—Parent participation. I. Elias, Jacquelyn. II. Mastroleo, Rosemary D. III. Title.

LC226.O44 2010
371.19'2—dc22   2009043860

This book is printed on acid-free paper.

10   11   12   13   14   10   9   8   7   6   5   4   3   2   1

Acquisitions Editor:	Cathy Hernandez
Editorial Assistant:	Sarah Bartlett
Production Editor:	Jane Haenel
Copy Editor:	Mark Bast
Typesetter:	C&M Digitals (P) Ltd.
Proofreader:	Cheryl Rivard
Indexer:	Sheila Bodell
Cover Designer:	Scott Van Atta

Contents

Preface

Research clearly demonstrates that the more parents are involved in their child's education, the more successful the student is. An essential key to parental involvement is the strength of the relationship between parents and the school.

Various professional articles speak to the need for strong parent-school relationships and many provide ideas and specific activities that can be employed to encourage parent involvement. However, few resources offer teaching and administrative professionals an in-depth look at how to forge strong relationships with parents and explore the issues and considerations needed to help build and maintain strong partnerships between home and school.

This book gives teachers and administrators the tools to build awareness of their own personalities and communication styles, understand those of the students and parents they are working with, and allow them to look at their constituents in a broader light so as to include parents more effectively in their child's education. Our goal is to help school personnel develop a broader understanding of the populations they serve and increase their sensitivity to the needs of students and their families. In addition, we provide teachers and administrators with ideas and strategies to develop better relationships with their students and families. If the relationships formed are more positive, parent involvement in school will increase. If parent involvement increases, student attendance, behavior, and academic achievement will improve.

This book is based on our extensive experience as public-school teachers and administrators. Additionally, we conducted a six-month anecdotal research study of parent feelings, perceptions, and relationships across several school districts. This study clarified and deepened our understandings of common issues and concerns that can make or break parent-school relationships. Our analysis of the study became the cornerstone of actual practices we put into place and are now presenting in this book. After identifying the common causes of both positive and negative parent-school relationships, we developed and successfully implemented a management plan for teachers and administrators to reduce the risk of negative relationships and build closer and more positive school-home connections.

OVERVIEW OF THE CHAPTERS

In the following chapters, we present guidelines and strategies to strengthen the school-home relationship, as well as actual situations to demonstrate effective and ineffective practices.

Chapter 1: Committing to the Relationship. The benefits of strong relationships between home and school to the child, teacher, parent, classroom, school, and school district are reviewed. Research is examined and anecdotal situations and results are provided to demonstrate how strong relationships between home and school made a significant difference in the education of the children involved.

Chapter 2: Recognizing Different Personalities. Personality inventories are discussed and one is offered as a tool to use with the stakeholders in the educational environment. How different personalities interact and how we might use our understanding of them to guide our actions is explored. Suggestions are offered to assist teachers and administrators in dealing with challenging parents and situations.

Chapter 3: Identifying Potential Red Flags. Specific situations and issues that impact school-home relationships are identified. A Likelihood Rating Scale is provided in which major issues that appear to impact the quality of school-home relationships are flagged. Suggested actions are provided to help reduce the negative impact of these factors on relationships between home and school.

Chapter 4: Honing Solid Communication Skills. Verbal and non-verbal communication obstacles are discussed. Strategies are offered to help school staff avoid these obstacles. In addition, proactive measures are offered for communicating in tense or conflict-ridden situations.

Chapter 5: Adopting Key Rules. Ten specific actions are identified that will significantly impact the quality of school-home relationships. These practices are discussed and examples are given to demonstrate how they lead to improved relationships.

Chapter 6: Using Flexibility to Enhance Relationships. Six situations are discussed that required school staff members to think outside the box and use flexibility with specific families. Examples of flexible solutions to challenging situations are provided for consideration and reflection.

Chapter 7: Documenting and Celebrating School Events. The importance of documenting school events and communicating those events to parents is discussed. Common ways to document and disseminate information are reviewed and some lesser-known or little-used strategies are offered to assist with school efforts to build and maintain positive ties to the home.

Chapter 8: Connecting Home and School. Three distinct levels of parent participation in schools are identified and discussed.

Chapter 9: Cultivating Resources. The need to cultivate outside resources for supporting families is overviewed. Strategies for building and providing a community network of support services are presented.

Chapter 10: Summarizing Global Lessons Learned. The big picture of what forges positive relationships between home and school is considered. Six critical behaviors are identified that, when demonstrated consistently and clearly, increase parents' positive feelings about the school and staff.

We encourage you to use this book as a basis for reflection. As you read, consider your own experiences and what the examples, stories, ideas, and strategies reveal about your relationships. Reflect on, analyze, dissect, and ponder your school-home connections and their impact on the level of parent involvement in your program. Begin by understanding why you must commit to building strong parent partnerships. Discover your own personal style and that of those around you, because personalities affect all of our relationships. Look for the warning signs of potential problems and fine-tune your communication skills, for communication is the key to our relationships. Build a repertoire of guidelines to follow, learn to be more flexible, find various avenues for parents to be involved, and document and celebrate your successes. Not only will students and parents benefit, but you stand to benefit as well. Since the quality of your school life depends on the quality of your school relationships, the development of more positive parental relationships will enrich your professional experience immensely.

Note: On the following pages, *I* refers to the primary author, Rosemary Olender. *We* refers to all three authors and our colleagues, who so willingly shared their work, stories, and insights.

Acknowledgments

I would like to acknowledge the personal relationship, camaraderie, and professional journey that Noreen M. Walker and I experienced together that brought me to writing this book. Noreen and I shared many years of schooling, social comradeship, and professional collegial positions as building administrators and then as directors of special education in neighboring school districts. Through our travails, we found common ground that led us to analyze our parental relationships for what was right and wrong. We embarked on an anecdotal study and made it our mission to talk to as many of our parents as we could, especially those who were not our best allies. From them, we learned the "dos" and "don'ts" that can make or break a relationship between home and school. Noreen, thank you for your friendship, your comradeship, and your personal and professional insights.

—Rosemary Olender

We would like to acknowledge Don Budmen, our legal mentor, and two of our closest colleagues who kept us on the straight and narrow and made sure we followed our own advice. To Don, Meg Vosburgh, and Donna Cooney, thank you. Your tireless efforts to keep us in good standing with our parents did not go unnoticed or unappreciated. We also acknowledge and thank those colleagues who shared their strategies, stories, thoughts, and ideas as part of our discourse. We especially need to thank our husbands, families, and friends, who lived through our celebrations and, more importantly, our frustrations and challenges throughout our professional lives.

We must acknowledge all of our students' parents, who have kept us honest and have worked with us through thick and thin. Without your responses, positive and negative, we would not have been able to analyze our successes and fix our mistakes.

Last, but not least, we need to make a special acknowledgment to a wonderful mentor and boss who paved the way toward making us

understand the importance of strong parental partnerships. To the late
Dr. Thomas P. O'Rourke, we thank you.

—Rosemary Olender, Jacquelyn Elias, and Rosemary Mastroleo

PUBLISHER'S ACKNOWLEDGMENTS

Corwin gratefully acknowledges the contribution of the following
individuals:

Patricia Bowman
Principal
C. Morley Sellery Special
    Education Center
Inglewood, CA

Mary Katherine Culver
Associate Professor,
    Clinical, of Educational
    Leadership
Northern Arizona University
Sierra Vista, AZ

Dolores M. Gribouski
Columbus Park School
Worcester, MA

Bruce Haddix
Principal
Center Grove Elementary
    School
Greenwood, IN

Sandra Harris
Professor of Educational
    Leadership
Lamar University
Beaumont, TX

Patrick M. Jenlink
Professor of Educational
    Leadership
Stephen F. Austin State
    University
Nacogdoches, TX

Richard Jones
Principal
John Adams Middle School
Rochester, MN

Barry Knight
Principal
Palmetto Middle School
Williamston, SC

Marianne Lucas Lescher
Principal
Kyrene de la Mariposa Elementary
    School
Gilbert, AZ

Michele Merkle
Principal
York Suburban High School
York, PA

Lyndon Oswald
Principal
Sandcreek Middle School
Idaho Falls, ID

Donald Poplau
Principal
Mankato East High School
Mankato, MN

Steve Reifman
Teacher
Santa Monica-Malibu USD
Santa Monica, CA

About the Authors

 **Rosemary A. Olender** is a retired school administrator who is currently providing consulting and staff development services for school districts across a broad range of educational issues. She has focused her work on the development of educational practices that lead to higher standards for all students and increased public relations between schools and communities. Ms. Olender received her bachelor's degree in speech pathology and audiology from the State University of New York at Albany, her master's degree in speech and language pathology from Syracuse University, and her CAS in educational administration from Syracuse University.

Prior to becoming an administrator, Ms. Olender taught for 17 years as a teacher (Grades 1–2, 7–9, 10–12) of profoundly deaf children in inclusive settings. She then became a general education administrator as associate principal for a junior high school (Grades 8–9) and principal of an elementary school (Grades K–4) before becoming director of special education (K–12) for the North Syracuse Central School District in upstate New York. She now focuses her consulting and staff development training for school districts and state organizations on a variety of topics centered on effective parent relations, inclusive practices, special education laws and practices, behavior management, and school-related personnel.

Ms. Olender is a member of the American Speech and Hearing Association, the Council of Exceptional Children, and the Association for Supervision and Curriculum Development. Additionally, she is a part-time administrator for the supervision of speech therapists providing Medicaid services in several upstate New York school districts.

Jacquelyn Elias is a retired speech therapist and school administrator residing in upstate New York. She received a bachelor of arts degree in speech pathology and audiology from the State University of New York at Geneseo and a master's and educational administrative degree from Oswego State University. Ms. Elias spent 19 years in the public schools as a speech therapist and special educator. Her primary interest was working with students with emotional disabilities and very young children with language disabilities.

Ms. Elias was a school administrator for 10 years. She spent three years as an intermediate school principal and seven years in the capacities of assistant director and director of special education programs in three different school districts. Ms. Elias was active in the NYSWA (New York State Women in Administration) organization and SAANYS (School Administrators Association of New York State).

Ms. Elias is now enjoying a new challenge as a stay-at-home mother of her 11-year-old daughter. Additionally, she takes pleasure in helping out in her home school district libraries and speech programs and volunteers community service time regularly as a member of a local telephone counseling program.

Rosemary D. Mastroleo is a retired schoolteacher and supervisor now living in Southwest Florida. Throughout her career, Ms. Mastroleo was responsible for the setup and design of special education programs in public-school settings. She focused her efforts on identifying the strengths and weaknesses of each child in order to build a successful academic program both at home and at school. Ms. Mastroleo's consistent efforts to build cooperative relationships with families enhanced the success of her students and her programs.

Prior to becoming an administrator, Ms. Mastroleo taught for 17 years in the North Syracuse Central School District in central New York. During that time, she was a first-grade teacher, an elementary counselor, a resource teacher, and then an itinerant junior and senior high school teacher. Following her tenure as a teacher, Ms. Mastroleo became a program monitor for the special education department in the North Syracuse District. Her duties included overseeing self-contained special education classes, sitting as a permanent member of the Committee on Special Education, and providing consultant services for special education and regular education teachers regarding students with special needs. In addition to her supervisory and consultant duties, Ms. Mastroleo became a hearing officer for the North Syracuse District during her last five years of service.

Committing to the Relationship

Programs designed with strong parent involvement produce students who perform better than otherwise identical programs that do not involve parents as thoroughly or that do not involve them at all.

—Anne T. Henderson

Why should schools work so hard to form and maintain positive parental relationships? In a nutshell, because research has clearly proven that student achievement improves when parents are involved in their child's education. So, in answer to the *why* question, the overwhelming answer is *increased student achievement*. It makes sense, then, since we are educators whose main goal is to help students learn and achieve, that we must believe in our obligation to forge strong relationships with the parents of our students.

A simple search of current and past literature on parent-school relationships will yield countless research reviews, books, and articles supporting the need for building strong relationships with parents and families. In a synthesis of 35 years of education research, Robert Marzano writes in *What Works in Schools* (2003) that community and parental involvement is one of 11 factors that are highly effective in enhancing student achievement. According to Henderson and Berla (1994), "The single best predictor of student success in school is the level of parental involvement in a child's education." The benefits of parental involvement include improved academic achievement, reduced absenteeism, improved school behavior, increased academic motivation, and lower dropout rates.

Henderson and Mapp (2002) found that regardless of family income or background, students whose parents are involved in their schooling are more likely to have higher grades and test scores. They also found that when parents are invested and participate in school activities, their children attend school regularly, develop better social skills, show improved behavior, and adapt well to school.

While the child's academic success is certainly the most important reason to build a strong, positive parent-teacher relationship, there are benefits that extend beyond those gained by the individual child. As parents and teachers forge strong ties, benefits expand to the teacher, parents, class, school, and, ultimately, the school district. Strong parent-teacher relationships can have a snowball effect on all stakeholders.

Henderson and Berla (1994) also found that, when parents participate in their child's school activities (e.g., volunteer readers, teacher assistants for special projects), the performance of not only their own child but that of all the children at school tends to improve. Additionally, they found that the more organized and comprehensive the partnership between parents and home, the higher the individual student academic achievement. Indeed, the presence of an additional adult in the classroom increases the amount and timeliness of direct attention the students receive and allows the teacher to focus on priority individual assistance where needed.

In reflecting on our personal experiences with the parents and families of our students, the evidence supporting the benefits of parental involvement is overwhelming. So much so that we often told parents that we needed their involvement, *even if* it was only to complain or to tell us that they were upset about something. We reminded them that it was their *job* to keep us on our toes, to keep us informed, and to advocate for their child. We referred to the educational process as "a three-part pie." One part is the student, one part is the school, and one part is the parent (i.e., home). We would further explain that "if one part spoils, the rest can go with it."

As we developed strong partnerships with parents, we began to observe numerous effects on the individual student, teacher, parent, classroom, school, and school district. A discussion of each follows, with some of the specific benefits we identified as we worked toward and developed strong parent-school relationships. We would encourage you, upon reflection of your own parental relationships, to think about observed and personally experienced benefits.

BENEFITS TO THE STUDENT

As proven, when the teacher and parent have a strong, positive relationship, student achievement improves. With collaboration and teamwork, we have observed that even with severe academic deficiencies, students show improvement when parents are involved.

As parents form a closer partnership, they tend to support school efforts at home with more frequency and intensity. This increased support leads to better achievement, which in itself becomes a strong rationale for putting in the time and effort to keep a child's parents involved. It supports taking action to do whatever is needed to forge a strong partnership.

Another observed benefit of a strong school-home partnership is that many children exhibit a sense of security in knowing that both their teacher and their parents are working together to help them do well in school. By working harmoniously, home and school can set clearer and more concise expectations for the child. They can also establish and maintain boundaries that are well articulated and consistent and form a collaborative team that creates solutions to problems that may arise. For sure, all of these possible outcomes will benefit the child academically, socially, and behaviorally. Don't underestimate the power of school and home alignment.

A commanding example of what happens when school and home are at odds is that of James, age 12. James was so used to his parents being angry with his teachers and school that he had little trust in any of the school staff. His parents' negativity and distrust were passed on to James to such a degree that he felt disloyal to his parents if he enjoyed a certain class or teacher. Consequently, he began to resist going to school. His behavior in school became defiant and oppositional. His teachers, in turn, felt frustrated and misunderstood, and they grew wary of communicating with James's parents at all. The situation only grew worse.

Only when a couple of James's teachers slowly and consistently called his parents with good reports of his abilities did an opening for change occur. Gradually, with a great deal of patience and understanding on the part of school personnel, James's parents became less combative and more receptive to hearing from the school. Over time, as the relationship improved between home and school, James started to relax, ended his resistance to attending school, became more cooperative, and made academic progress.

Other benefits to the student include the following:

- Increased motivation
- Lower absenteeism

- Decreased use of drugs and alcohol
- Fewer suspensions
- Improved attitude
- Increased cooperation

BENEFITS TO THE TEACHER

Strong parent-teacher relationships have several advantages in addition to those enjoyed by the students. When teachers have positive relationships with students' parents, understanding of and support for classroom curriculum and activities rises. Collaboration often leads to improved ideas, enriched resources (e.g., volunteers, donations), expanded trust, and increased teacher willingness to try new things. All of these, in turn, lead to improved teacher confidence, job satisfaction, and self-esteem.

Through our discussions with and observations of teachers who had strong, positive relationships with parents, several noticeable commonalities appeared. In general, these teachers employed a more positive, nurturing approach to their instruction. They appeared to have more energy and less stress. They brought *home* into the discussion and made the school an extension of the child's life with his or her family. They increased the relevance of what students learned in school by sharing family situations and stories that were pertinent to the educational discussion. The teachers were seemingly happier with their job and provided classrooms that were positively charged.

In general, teachers who forge strong partnerships with parents and families enjoy higher levels of student achievement, professional license to try new things, and personal satisfaction with their day-to-day activities. We know how draining a negative or hostile parental relationship can be to our teaching. It makes the benefits of working hard to turn that negative into a positive all the more worth it.

Other benefits to the teacher include the following:

- Fewer discipline problems
- Increased time to focus on task at hand
- Greater sense of value to the classroom and school
- Decreased sense of isolation in their work
- Improved job satisfaction

BENEFITS TO THE PARENT

The most valuable parental benefit of having a positive relationship with their child's teacher is the development of trust that emerges from this relationship. As parents' trust in their child's teacher increases, their anxieties tend to decrease. As their anxieties decrease, their willingness to support the efforts of the teacher increases. This, in turn, increases their child's academic achievement.

Another benefit of this forged relationship is the sense of partnership built in the educational process. This partnership can empower parents and increase their sense of ownership in their child's education. As their sense of ownership increases, their commitment to school events, activities, and requests for support will likewise increase. This commitment will lead to their own personal satisfaction and involvement in their child's education.

As the relationship develops in a positive fashion, parents will enjoy a higher level of comfort with the teacher. This will lead to a more honest and open sharing of information that is critical to the child's overall well-being and success in school. Parents will feel supported and assisted in their desires to have their child thrive in school.

Other benefits to parents include the following:

- Additional information source for potentially problematic family issues with negative educational effects
- Additional support for family initiatives that may need carryover outside the home (e.g., diet and health programs)
- Greater security in knowing that the child's educational needs are recognized and addressed
- A child who views school in a more positive light

BENEFITS TO THE CLASS

As previously stated, when parents have positive relationships with teachers, they tend to become more involved in school activities. As their involvement increases, they offer more experiences to share with the class. They will be more likely to volunteer their services for special events or for in-class activities such as tutoring or aide programs in the classroom. Additional support in the classroom is of benefit to all.

Since the collective mind is always better than the single mind, increased parental involvement leads to increased ideas and creativity for instruction. It is easier to establish the class as a community and allow the teacher to stay focused on the instruction while the parents take care of the extraneous duties to carry out the instructional plan (e.g., finding or setting up materials for activities).

Having another set of eyes in the classroom can be of great help to the entire class. If the teacher requests assistance with observing anything specific in the classroom, the parent may lend a unique perspective that can be most helpful to the teacher, who can't always see everything that is happening while focusing on instruction. The parent might even come up with some suggestions or ideas that will benefit the class or aid in the delivery of instruction.

One case in point involved a volunteer parent who consistently assisted in writing class. She noticed that a small group of students who were not strong writers were consuming a great deal of the teacher's time in getting started on their writing pieces. This caused the teacher to work less efficiently with stronger writers who still needed support with mechanics. The parent, working with the stronger writers, noticed that they got off to a quicker start because they could generate ideas faster for their writing pieces. The parent suggested pairing stronger writers with weaker ones to generate writing ideas, allowing both teacher and parent to work with all students on the mechanics of the writing samples being generated. The teacher accepted and used the suggestion very successfully from that time on.

Other benefits to the class include the following:

- Wider exposure to cultural differences represented by families
- Increased attention to each student with better student-adult ratio
- Increased on-task behavior
- Introduction of additional ideas and experiences to the curriculum

BENEFITS TO THE SCHOOL

Strong, positive relationships between parents and teachers build trust in the entire school. This trust reaps significant positive public relations, which can then translate to support of schoolwide initiatives. We all know the benefits of having a strong, supportive parental group working toward the school's goals.

Strong, positive relationships between parents and teachers also serve to open the lines of communication and apprise administrators of important issues and concerns that parents may have about the school. By receiving this information from parents, administrators can work proactively to address concerns or solve current problems brought to their attention. Concurrently, by listening to many parents, administrators can assess what is enjoyed and valued by the parental community.

With increased parental trust and school support, the success of school goals and objectives is enhanced.

Other benefits to the school include the following:

- Increased recruitment of highly qualified personnel because of positive parental support
- More positive school climate
- Increased community support for activities and initiatives

BENEFITS TO THE SCHOOL DISTRICT

The positive public relations that come with strong parent-school relationships yield many benefits to the school district. Districts that are viewed positively become common knowledge in the areas in which they reside. Districts that enjoy a positive image in their local communities typically attract homeowners and the attention of local businesses and groups. Community agencies are frequently looking for sites to offer their services, and many of these services can help support school efforts. District partnerships with local agencies provide a win-win situation for both.

It's no secret that money for education is a national issue. Different states use different sources of school funding. However, regardless of the funding source, schools with higher achievement rates, higher levels of parental and community support, or both are more likely to receive what they need to continue their programs.

In our state, New York, money for school districts comes from property owners, and most budgets are voted on by the constituents of the district. In this situation, strong, positive relationships with parents will yield stronger support for the schools and an increased likelihood that the annual budgets will be passed.

Other benefits to the district include the following:

- Collective support for long-range referendums
- Good recruitment and retention of highly qualified staff
- Improved property values due to desirable education system

As we reflect on the relationships we have had with parents over the years, one observation becomes absolutely clear. The more committed you are to working with parents and forging relationships between home and school, and the more positive those relationships become, the more successful and satisfying your work will be. Engaging parents in welcoming and valuable ways provides them with ownership in the educational process. Ownership leads to support and value for what is happening.

Parents and teachers must work together to support the development of the student at home and school. In forming strong collaborations, we not only help the individual student, we help ourselves, our classroom, our school, and our district. Ultimately, the school community is strengthened.

SUMMARY

Educational research demonstrates strong support of the need for active parent involvement in their children's education. The benefits are numerous and extend beyond those to the students themselves. As we reviewed our personal observations and experiences over the years, it became obvious that everyone involved in a student's education benefitted from parental involvement in our schools.

The greater the collaboration between parents, teachers, and schools, the greater the benefits to the student, teacher, classroom, school, and the entire district. It is critical that teachers and administrators commit to forming positive relationships with parents and families to enhance student achievement, improve attendance and motivation, decrease behavioral problems, and facilitate school and district initiatives requiring community support.

Recognizing Different Personalities

The most important ingredient we put into any relationship is not what we say or what we do but what we are.

—Stephen R. Covey

Your personality affects your relationships. Likewise, the personalities of the people you encounter on a daily basis affect the relationship they will have with you. One of the key components of a successful relationship is the ability to understand both your own and the other person's perspective. Another is to respect individual differences. A third is to capitalize on each other's strengths. Because of these components, relationships rely heavily on the nature of the personalities involved. Positive relationships are built on trust and rapport, and they require some basic understanding of the likenesses and differences of the personalities involved. There are many books and inventories on personality types; how they fit together, how they may complement or clash with each other, and how to cope with or handle different personalities. Understanding your own personality type and the types of those you are involved with adds a component that can be very useful in forging strong relationships between home and school.

When people understand each other's underlying personality styles, it is easier to understand their behaviors and differing points of view. It becomes easier to adjust your communication style to meet their needs and approach them in a way that is not as threatening or disconcerting as it might otherwise have been. Compromises are more easily facilitated and communication improves. Taking the time to understand yourself and others you have to live, work, or deal with can bring great benefits to the working relationship and will allow for similarities and differences to be explored and understood.

DETERMINING PERSONALITY

As educators, you have most likely taken one or more personality inventories in the development of your career. Through these inventories, you have probably discovered whether or not you are a "leader," "intuitive," an "introvert," "extrovert," or other classification. Based on Carl Jung's 1923 theories, Isabel Myers and her mother, Katharine Briggs, developed a personality test, which was first published in 1962. The MBTI (Myers-Briggs Type Indicator) focuses on normal populations and emphasizes the value of naturally occurring differences. While Myers-Briggs is one of the most popular inventories, it is important to note that there are others that can also be used to provide you with an understanding of the basic personality types that exist in personal, professional, and social situations.

In our quest to develop and facilitate positive relationships, we have found that an excellent personality inventory developed by Gary Smalley and John Trent (see Resource A) can be extremely useful in understanding your own basic personality and those of your colleagues, students, and their parents. We have used a modified version of their personality test (see Resource B). This test provides a quick assessment tool that can discern four basic personality profiles.

In a nutshell, Smalley and Trent break the general population into four basic personality types. To help people easily remember the key characteristics of the types, they correspond with four different animals—the lion, otter, golden retriever, and beaver. To determine their type, participants complete a short questionnaire, which takes about five to ten minutes. They then score their answers to determine their basic personality type, as well as to identify which traits or characteristics of the other three types are more or less prevalent in their personality. Awareness of these four basic personalities helps people understand how they may relate to and impact each other in a working relationship.

Over the years, we have given this test to countless teachers, administrators, students, friends, and family members. In over 100 group administrations, rarely have participants disagreed with their own findings. A vast majority have agreed to a large extent with not only their own findings but with the findings of others in the group who they had personal or professional relationships with. Sharing the results among the groups has led to lengthy discussions and analyses of how specific actions or situations may have been tied to personality types. These analyses, in turn, often led to greater understanding and improved communication between participants.

In one setting, the test was administered to an entire school of teachers, teaching assistants, administrators, and support personnel. The results of the test led to an animated discussion of a particularly tough situation the school was facing and how the different types were helping or delaying resolution to the situation. After several minutes of discussion, it was decided that the resolution to the problem would come from assigning different tasks to different people in a manner that would suit their personality types and allow for the work of each to complement the others. The superintendent informed me four months later that the process had been a highly successful one, and the situation had been resolved to everyone's satisfaction. Additionally, he told me that the relationships between staff members had improved, and talk in the break rooms often returned to discussions of the animal personality types.

On one occasion, I used the test with my entire family at a holiday gathering. At first I got the usual roll of the eyes and "do we have to?" from the group. I assured them it would take only five minutes of their time, so they agreed to go along with my activity. But once they did the test, no one left the table, and we actually sat for more than an hour discussing each other's basic traits and how we needed to understand each other's style and needs better. No one was surprised with anyone else's results, but now we had a better understanding of how to deal with each other in a more positive way. As a result, there have been more positive discussions, fewer arguments, more considerations extended, and less personalizing of each other's actions.

We have provided you with an adapted version of the test to facilitate an easy assessment process (Resource B). Column 1 of the test suggests the lion personality, Column 2 the otter, Column 3 the golden retriever, and Column 4 the beaver. Once you tally the totals of each column, Resource C will give you the characteristics of each animal and identify its prevalent traits.

We suggest you simply give people the inventory (Resource A) without discussing the four personality types in advance. Once users have completed the inventory, discuss the four types, column by column, and identify the traits of each animal.

EFFECTS OF PERSONALITIES ON YOUR RELATIONSHIPS

For discussion purposes, and for an understanding of how personality types might mesh, we'd like to use the Smalley types and explore how your parental relationships might be affected by the personalities involved. The interpersonal dynamics might be better understood and viewed in a more positive fashion if underlying personality styles are recognized.

As mentioned above, Smalley and Trent use four animals to represent four personality types—the lion, otter, golden retriever, and beaver. The "lion" personality is a dominant figure that has vision, is highly productive, strong-willed, independent, and very much a leader. Weaknesses may include a domineering, unforgiving, cold demeanor at times. People with "otter" personalities are influential, outgoing, responsive, friendly, compassionate, and make good "second lieutenants" or followers. They find ways around obstacles to get things accomplished. On the other hand, their weaknesses lie in sometimes operating in an undisciplined and unproductive manner. People who fit the "golden retriever" profile are steady, calm, easygoing, and very dependable. Their weaknesses lie in their need for constancy and fear of change. They can be fearful and indecisive. "Beaver" personalities are analytical, organized, industrious, and self-disciplined. Their weaknesses lie in their tendencies to become negative and touchy or unsociable. For more information about the personality profiles, see Resource C.

Working with lion parents can be especially trying. They like to be in charge and need control. They are highly determined individuals who are persistent, strong-willed, and bold. They express their opinions strongly and, often, forcefully. If you understand this, and recognize them as the lions they are, it can attenuate your compulsion to take it personally and feel victimized, especially if you're a golden retriever! If you are a lion yourself, you need to work out who is in charge and when and find ways to relinquish control where you can. If you are an otter, you can flex and find ways around the issues at hand to maintain the goals you have set out. If you are a beaver, you'll need to stifle your desire to attack when pressured.

Parents who are otters should be less demanding to work with. Because of their flexibility, enthusiasm, and generally friendly nature, relationships are not as easily strained. They will usually allow you more leeway to try new things and be optimistic about your plans. Use these parents to rally the other parents, to share their insights, ideas, and suggestions with you. They will probably command more time from you with their verbal nature and desire to work in groups.

Be mindful of your golden retriever parents' sensitivity. While loyal and not very demanding, these are the parents who you can upset easily if they sense their child has been wronged or your communications are viewed negatively. Changes in routine will distress them, but they may not let you know you have upset them. They will avoid conflict and keep their feelings inside until they explode. If you are a lion, be especially mindful of your ability to destroy their confidence or push them away from being involved in their child's education.

Beaver parents should, for the most part, be predictable. They can be of great help to you with activities that need organizing, attention to detail, and precise scheduling. They tend to make great PTO (Parent-Teacher Organization) representatives and room parents. They take directions well and are good at gathering information and facts. Be careful, however, not to provoke them. They can respond with persistent, deliberate, fact-filled reactions that can be difficult to deflect.

IMPLICATIONS

If you decide to use the inventory with staff, parents, or both, you will want to discuss how the four basic personalities work to complement each other, how they might interact with each other, and how understanding one's type and the types of others can help each of you to understand how to best work together. Resource C provides additional information about the four types.

It is important to recognize that each of us has traits from all four personalities. Some of us may be predominantly represented in one or two types, while holding some or minimal characteristics of the others. I have administered this profile to literally hundreds of teachers and administrators over the past 10 years. Responses to the inventory results are consistently predictable. Rarely have I found more than one or two members of the audience who disagree with the type their profile suggests. When I review the traits of golden retrievers, owners of these animals laugh and verify that their dogs actually behave in ways that fit the profile. Beavers identify themselves as the obsessive-compulsive ones. Lions admit they want to be in charge and are not happy when they are not. Otters laugh, and their colleagues verify that they are, indeed, the ones who always see the glass as half full and find the humor in any situation. Essentially, the veracity of the inventory has been demonstrated repeatedly.

It is the interplay of these personality types that can be an advantage or disadvantage to a particular relationship or specific situation. For example, two lions could understandably come into conflict if both want control or feel the need to take the lead. Lions, when aggressive, can easily dominate and hurt a golden retriever in a difficult situation. Beavers can frustrate and anger a lion who needs to get the job done quickly. Yet it is precisely the marriage of the traits from all four that can make for a successful relationship. The goal is to be mindful of the basic personality type you are dealing with and understand how your own type relates to it and other personalities.

The beauty of forming relationships and working as an "education team" is that all four personality types can be valuable to the work at hand. There is no one type that is "better" or "worse" than another. This inventory will simply allow you to better understand your own traits and behaviors as well as those of coworkers and family members. By using the knowledge of the different traits, you will have more information to let you forge more positive relationships with these different types.

Schools have reported to me months and even years later that their staffs continue to use their knowledge of these personality types to analyze the interpersonal incidences that occur in their school (and home) life. They have told me that as a result of having a better understanding of basic personality types, they can look at situations more objectively and empathize with where someone might be coming from. They use the profiles to delegate tasks and rely on the strengths of each other to work collaboratively. Most importantly, they use the profiles to be more empathetic and patient with the traits and needs of the different types.

John and Cindy Trent and Gary and Norma Smalley wrote a wonderful book titled *The Treasure Tree* (1992) that offers information on how these personalities work together. This book can be used with all ages and is an excellent way to introduce the topic of animal personalities to a class. Some teachers have read the book and then given the inventory to their class, discussed the animal types with the students, and used it in classroom discussions throughout the year. One teacher reported that arguments and disagreements between her students significantly dropped once the students were able to analyze initial differences in reactions that were arising. Their acceptance of the basic differences led to more positive relationships between members of the class.

By simply understanding these four personality types and the behaviors that each tends to exhibit, you will have some important clues about the individuals you are dealing with. Informally, you can probably guess what personality type someone might be without using the formal inventory. However, actually using the inventory with students, parents, or both can be of great benefit to the teacher and the parent in the initial stages of developing a relationship. Having the parent understand the four basic types, as well as your own type, can help them to understand your basic style and how to collaborate with you. Knowing the personality types of parents and their children can be of great help in dealing with school and home issues that arise.

It is important to note that you can't change another person. Knowing their basic personality type merely allows you to understand where they are coming from and how they might react to a situation, approach an issue, or attack a problem you might present. Likewise, understanding their basic personality will give you some clues about how you might need to approach them given their personality traits. Keep in mind that psychological typing is not universally accepted and should never be too rigidly accepted. Use this simply as one tool in your arsenal of relationship-forging strategies.

DEALING WITH DIFFICULT PARENTS

As educators, you have had to deal with many different personality types among your parents. From your experience, you know that some parents are very involved, positive, and supportive, while we never see or hear from other parents regardless of the measures we take to get them involved. Now let's talk about how we should deal with those difficult and involved parents, as well as those we must connect with but who are very difficult to contact.

What is meant by a *difficult* parent? Some parents seem to be overinvolved and may consistently question your teaching strategies, course content, homework, discipline procedures, grading process, and so on. They may go directly to your principal with their grievances or questions without talking with you directly. Or they may say nothing until they are filled with concern or frustration and explode with a host of issues for you to deal with.

Another difficult parent to deal with is one who is very general with opinions or comments and simply complains about the overall nature of your teaching, homework, or discipline. This type does not offer specifics, and it is very difficult to ascertain the problem causing the parent's frustration with you or the school. You are merely on the receiving end of the criticism and overall negative feelings that the parent might display.

Some difficult parents let you know, in no uncertain terms, that they know everything there is to know about the curriculum, grade level, proper disciplinary techniques, and the type and quantity of homework that should be given. Often, these parents are teachers themselves and have teaching styles or strategies that differ from your own.

Finally, we must add the uninvolved parent to the list of difficult parents. While it might seem that these parents are easier to deal with, in reality, they are not. If we believe that a parent's involvement in his or her child's education is important to the child's success, then dealing with parents who are not involved is, indeed, dealing with difficult parents. Finding ways to get them involved may not be easy, but it is essential.

In a future chapter, we will talk about how to deal with parents who may not be involved due to cultural, economic, or situational factors. For the purposes of this chapter, let's just add to our list those parents who are not involved due to their own personality styles. Parents who are unresponsive or who want to avoid conflict will delay dealing with the school if they think they will find, or have already had, negative interactions with the school. Additionally, we need to consider other parents who don't want to disagree with anything and are willing to just go with the flow and accept whatever happens. In essence, these are the golden retrievers of our parent set. They can be problematic because we will not know what their true concerns or feelings are. This may lead to problems if we make false assumptions and take actions based on a lack of information or inaccurate assumptions.

So what are some general guidelines that can be used in difficult situations and interactions with parents? How can we capitalize on our interactions from an interpersonal-actions approach and reduce negativity? Essentially, by following these conventions as much as possible:

- Stay calm and assess the situation objectively, without emotions.
- Provide facts with honesty and clarity.
- Be likeable.
- Don't take things personally.
- Don't make assumptions.
- Be sincere and do not criticize.
- Be proactive in your establishment of the relationship.
  - Smile.
  - Listen carefully and actively to what they say.
  - Become interested in them as a person.
  - Find common goals and interests.
  - Compliment them when legitimate.
  - Make them feel important to the process or issue.
  - Find *positive* interactions to engage in with them.

We know that the above actions may sound easy but will, in the midst of the situation, be hard to apply. It is especially difficult to adhere to these conventions when the situation is highly negative or emotionally charged. So how do we keep ourselves calm in the face of a blood-pressure-raising situation? How do we calm the other person(s)? Let's turn to brain research for ideas.

Research on cerebral hemispheric dominance (Ornstein, 1997) strongly supports that we have two sides to our brain that, while they work in concert with each other through the corpus callosum, have distinctly different characteristics. Our right side, or "right brain," houses our emotions. It is the side that is creative, intuitive, colorful, and emotional. To the contrary, the left side of our brain, or "left brain," holds the logical, analytical, orderly, problem-solving, rational part of our being. Ideally, we can utilize both sides most of the time. However, an interesting thing happens when we become highly emotional (i.e., pushed far into the right brain). The more we are hunkered down in that side, the less we can access the left brain—our rational side.

It stands to reason, then, that when we are in a highly emotional state (hanging out in our right brain, so to speak) and need to think or act in a problem-solving or rational manner (use our left brain), we might need to jump-start a "switch" to activate our left brain. To do that, we need to calm ourselves down. While easier said than done in the midst of the situation, there are some specific actions we can take that will do just that— push us to the other side.

The old adage to "count to 10" is precisely one way to get to and stay in the left brain. In fact, employing any rote task (e.g., counting to 10, thinking of days of the week or months of the year in sequential order, taking notes of the conversation) will push us to the analytical side of our brain and dampen the emotional side that wants to let loose! Looking up also has that effect. When on the phone (because you do not want the other person to see you do this), keeping your head static and rolling your eyes up to the ceiling for several seconds will bring a similar result and allow you to calm down.

Getting someone else into their left brain, however, is a bit more complicated. It's doable but more complicated. The first thing you must do is remain calm yourself (or get yourself into the left-brain mode first). Another basic rule of thumb is to listen attentively *without interruption*. The reason you must not interrupt is that the act of interruption itself pushes the emotional person further into their right brain!

Another tactic is to make an empathic statement. For example, you might say, "I can hear how frustrated (angry, concerned, confused, fearful) you are and can understand why you might be feeling the way you do." However, be very sure that you are really listening and are sincere in your empathy. Nothing can destroy a relationship faster than the perception that you are being insincere and merely placating the person who is being emotional. Adding personal agreement can be of help also.

Forming questions or statements that end in the word *first* will also help to calm people and move them into their left brain. For example, asking "What would you like me to do *first?*" or stating "We have several options. Here's what I suggest we do first, then second" are powerful ways to put the conversation into an analytical, hence left-brained, arena.

I can recall one highly charged incident in my office. A parent of a junior high school student stormed past my secretary and into my office yelling loudly and demanding to see me immediately. She had been called by the school principal and told that her son was being suspended because he had used foul language in the classroom. Her son had thrown the *F*-bomb in his science class, and his teacher threw him out of class and sent him to the dean. He was then sent to the principal and given a three-day suspension.

What is important to note here is that her son had Tourette syndrome and that using the *F* word, while more under control at the time of the event, was still a manifestation of his disability. His mother was understandably upset and fully ready to contact her lawyer about her son's rights being violated. Since I was in the position to oversee the actions taken with disabled students, she headed directly to me after she slammed the phone on the principal.

I asked her to wait just a moment for me to clear my schedule so that I could give her my full attention. I then allowed her to vent her anger and frustration for several minutes without interruption and responded with, "Wow! No wonder you are spitting mad! I can understand your frustration and I will help you deal with this. The first thing I need to do is to call the principal and get a full description of the incident that occurred in the classroom. Then, we have two options open for us to explore." By using the words *first* and *two options*, I pressed her to consider an orderly approach, thereby moving her out of her right brain somewhat and into her left brain. She did calm down enough for us to problem solve who would do what, when we would accomplish the tasks, and what outcomes we would be looking for.

SUMMARY

Relationships are affected by personality and communication styles. Understanding your own personality type and considering those of others with whom you interact will add an important dynamic that can enhance and facilitate more positive communications. Relationships change over time and with varied experiences, so you need to work at keeping them sound.

It is easy to maintain a positive relationship when personalities complement each other and issues or situations are positive. It is when the personalities clash or when our interests or perspectives differ from others that we tend to lose patience and enthusiasm, and, if not careful, make major communication blunders that could cost us the relationship for a long time, if not forever.

Take the time to complete a personality inventory if you have not already done so. Analyze your own style and reflect on how that style may be affecting the relationships around you. Then, once you have an understanding of your own basic personality style, proceed with the following strategies:

- Observe and try to decipher the personality types of those you are dealing with—or find venues to actually administer a basic inventory.
- Consider the implications of the types of personalities involved and their interplay on your relationships.
- Build a "bank" of strategies to use with different personalities, particularly those needed to employ with parents who question everything you do, challenge your teaching practices, do "end runs" around you to your principal, or are not involved until their frustration level escalates to the point of confrontation.
- Try to remain as calm as possible in heated situations and tap into your left brain so that emotions are kept in check.
- Use strategies to help calm others down and think more logically and analytically, without emotional overload.

Identifying Potential Red Flags

The pessimist sees difficulty in every opportunity. The optimist sees the opportunity in every difficulty.

—Winston Churchill

RECOGNIZING RED FLAGS

When dealing with the multitude of parents who place their children in your care, one of the most important things you can do is to learn to recognize any obstacles or "red flags" that might get raised. These flags will serve to warn you of a potentially difficult relationship with a parent that may form a stumbling block to building trust and a positive relationship with the school.

Over the years, experiences with many different families and parents have brought to light common themes that ultimately turn out to be red flags signaling oncoming problems. Working with colleagues from different school districts, it seemed that our "war stories" held many common themes and often led to similar outcomes. Because this intrigued me, I decided to do some research that allowed me to identify, highlight, and articulate what some of the common conditions were that could lead to problematic school-home relationships.

I asked for, and had the good fortune to be granted, a six-month sabbatical from my position as a school administrator. While on sabbatical,

I began to investigate, with my friend and colleague Noreen Walker, what situations, conditions, beliefs, and experiences shaped the attitudes that our parents brought with them when meeting with school personnel. We conducted a series of paper surveys, listening sessions, and individual and small-group interviews with parents, teachers, and administrators. Once this information had been gathered, we then conducted "situational autopsies" to determine the most common factors that influenced parental attitudes and the level of parental cooperation we were experiencing. The similarity of responses from parent to parent, regardless of district, was amazing. An analysis of all of our data was completed. We combined the collective experiences of those we interviewed, and from that, we were able to identify important indicators of positive and negative conditions impacting the type of relationships parents had with their child's teachers and school communities.

THE LIKELIHOOD RATING SCALE

In analyzing our data, we were able to create a Likelihood Rating Scale. This scale can be used as a tool to assist teachers and administrators in assessing the possible factors that may increase or decrease the likelihood of problems arising with specific parents and families. Understanding what factors may be contributing to the problem, and taking actions to address them, can lower the risk of problems interfering with the desired school-home collaboration.

Because we recognized early on that it was not simply *family* conditions that could increase the likelihood of problems, our research went beyond the questioning of scores of parents. Teachers and administrators often bring their own "conditions" that likewise increase the potential for sabotaging the development of a cooperative and productive school-home relationship. Therefore, we met with dozens of teachers and school administrators and offer you the common indicators of problems arising from those two groups as well.

We devised a rating system for your use that is a simple scale from *less likely* to *more likely*. The more the identified condition exists or is perceived to exist (i.e., the higher you rate its occurrence), the more likely the presence of problems between home and school. Conversely, the less the condition exists (i.e., the lower you rate its occurrence), the less likely it is that there will be problems, and the relationship between home and school will likely be stronger. Conditions that impact the relationship will be identified, and suggestions to alleviate and address the conditions are offered for your consideration.

PARENT AND FAMILY CONDITIONS

Less Likely _____ More Likely

| 1 | 2 | 3 | 4 | 5 |

1. Parents Who Lack Confidence in the Teacher's or District's Intent to Help Their Child

Again and again parents told us of specific incidences that had taken place, or of statements that teachers or administrators had made, that convinced them that their child "didn't matter." These parents felt that "the rules," past history, and a desire to treat everyone the same took precedence and trumped their individual child's needs. They did not trust the teachers or administrators to care about their child.

Trust is vital to the success of any relationship. Parents must believe and trust that the teacher and school genuinely care about and are willing to do whatever is necessary to help their child. Breaches in this trust can be costly, and it takes only one instance or an uncaring remark or response to erode this trust.

Trust builders include the following:

- Articulating and demonstrating your concern for each child and your intent to help each child succeed
- Demonstrating individualized efforts to assist the child with academic and personal problems
- Taking the time to understand the child's unique skills and areas of weakness that need to be addressed
- Sharing with parents your understanding of their child and his or her needs
- Allowing parents the time or venue they need to express their thoughts; teachers need to talk less, ask questions, and listen more

2. Parents Who Lack a Support System for Home Issues

Many families are facing challenging economic, health, cultural, relational, and environmental difficulties. This makes it more difficult for them to stay involved in a positive way with the schools. Schools cannot resolve most family problems.

We can, however, be a solid resource for information to which parents can turn. We have the ability to provide many family resources (e.g., social workers, therapists, entertainment programs), but we cannot provide all that is needed. What we *can* do, however, is provide parents with as much information as feasible that can be used to assist them in finding the resources they need for support with ongoing home issues.

It will be very helpful and supportive to offer families information on the following:

- Local and county agencies that can assist with pressing family issues such as childcare, housing, mental health, and health insurance
- State and federal agencies and programs that can help families with financial or legal situations
- Local organizations that connect families with their cultural base

3. Parents Who Have Not Established a Trusting Relationship With at Least One District Employee

A significant indicator of negative relationships and a breakdown between school and home was identified by parents who felt that they had not been able to establish a trusting relationship with *any* district employee. They trusted no one and nothing the district did. On the other hand, parents who were wary but still gave the benefit of the doubt, despite several negative instances, named at least one person they trusted. This trust then led to a significantly reduced likelihood of problems. It appears that as long as at least one district person establishes a trusting relationship, the likelihood of a more positive connection is increased.

Sometimes, it takes just one individual to open the doors of communication and help build the connections needed to benefit the child. You can be the person who establishes the trusting relationship. If you don't succeed, despite your many efforts, find someone else in the child's school day who can make a home connection and have *them* start to build trust. Don't rule out the following individuals, who might be able to establish a connection and build at least the start of a trusting relationship:

- School administrator
- School nurse
- Custodian (yes, they sometimes have the ear of parents)

- Another teacher
- Teaching assistant
- Librarian
- PTO president or active member
- Another parent who *does* trust you

4. Parents Who Have Not Moved Beyond the Denial Stage in the Grief Process

Parents whose children struggle academically or socially in school (particularly if their child is diagnosed with a disability) experience a sense of loss or grief and are often stuck in the denial stage of the grief process. Many deny that their children have problems. Many times blame is placed on the teacher, class, another student, administration, or rules. As long as they deny the problem, the likelihood of a more positive relationship is lowered.

Teachers and administrators have to honor the reality of parents in the grief process. They need to let the parents know that it is just that, a *process*, which takes time and can't be hurried. Teachers need to allow that time, provide empathy, listen actively, and not expect the parent to just "get over it."

Parents need support and help to move beyond the denial stage. They can make progress if you do the following:

- Listen carefully and try to understand whether they have recognized or accepted the problem.
- Find the strengths of the child and lead with a discussion of those strengths.
- Objectively outline the problem as it exists.
- Objectively articulate how the problem presents itself (be the camera, not the commentator) and explain how the situation looks.
- Offer suggestions and a plan to remediate the problem.
- Provide support and assistance with the remediation process.
- *Don't* place blame on either the child or the family.
- Connect the parent with other parents who have moved through the grief process individually or through a support group.
- Provide education about their child's difficulties or disability.

5. Family Members Who Do Not Agree With Each Other on Educational or Disciplinary Issues

The likelihood of a positive collaboration with the home is significantly diminished if there is conflict within the family about what the school issues are. This is a tough issue to address without working directly with the parties who disagree. Our natural inclination is to stay out of the disagreement, but that doesn't help the relationship needed to enhance the education of the child.

Some suggestions for steps or activities that might help resolve this conflict are the following:

- Meeting with the disagreeing parties separately to explain the issues, hear their views, and ask questions
- Meeting with the disagreeing parties jointly to mediate a discussion of the issues
- Having a mutually agreed-upon third party present at confrontational meetings (e.g., another teacher, an administrator, or family friend)
- Clearly articulating in an objective manner the issues and possible solutions to the disagreement, with parental input
- Agreeing to disagree and come back to evaluate the situation at a later date
- Maintaining the best relationship you can with each party, understanding that one may be better than the other

6. Parents Who Are Not Able to Change Preconceived Notions

Sometimes, parents have made up their minds about what or how their child will be taught or how they will be disciplined in school. They have preconceived notions that will not allow them to compromise or negotiate situations that they feel are not fair or warranted. Examples include those parents who feel that they can dictate homework rules and standards, challenge all grades given, or interfere with their child's classes. One common notion is that teachers "work for parents," and, therefore, parents can and should challenge anything that the teacher or school does that they disagree with.

Accept the fact that you may not be able to change some preconceived notions that stand in the way of a better relationship with that parent or family. If you've tried and haven't succeeded, keep the following in mind:

- Don't take it personally. It has much more to do with them and their past experiences than it does with you specifically.
- Try to understand where they are coming from. Ask *why* they feel the way they do in an objective, fact-finding matter. This might help you to empathize with their stand, even if you do not agree with them. It might also give you some idea of how to compromise or negotiate a solution to the problem at hand, if possible.

7. Parents Who Are Not Knowledgeable About Their Child's Educational Needs

Many parents recognize that their child has an academic, behavioral, or emotional problem (sometimes a disability), but they do not fully understand the ramifications or impact of the problem on their child's academic and social success. They hear all the words we use (e.g., *unmotivated, learning disability, hyperactive, unfocused, motor delay, low tolerance*), but they truly do not comprehend all of the ways in which that problem interferes with the learning process.

We cannot assume that they *should* know or have been told of the problem prior to our working with their child. We need to know what they do and don't already know. Then we need to clarify information so that the working relationship that evolves will enhance our efforts to help the child succeed. Some simple ways to provide information to parents include the following:

- Have face-to-face discussions with clear descriptions of how the problems are manifested in the classroom and affect the learning process, with examples given.
- Provide written materials about the types of problems the child has.
- Provide Web sites that might assist the parent in learning more about the problems their child faces.
- Provide local resources that could assist the parent when dealing with problems and issues that involve the home (e.g., doctors, counselors, support groups).

8. Parents Who Are Not Able or Willing to Incorporate Educational Recommendations

As we encounter increasing numbers of families with diverse needs, we often meet a family that simply cannot provide ample support at home for school recommendations. Homework poses significant challenges for many families who have extremely busy or chaotic lives that truly interfere with their ability to work with their child on any kind of a regular basis.

As you know, many of our families today have not learned or are not yet fluent in English. Therefore, many are unable to comprehend the letters and papers that come home, making them incapable of helping their child even if they want to. This can be particularly difficult for those isolated parents who speak a language that is not well represented in the community. Others, with or without language difficulties, may simply be incapable of understanding what is being asked (e.g., course content is too abstract).

Some families simply feel that school issues are for school and home issues are for home, and never the twain shall meet. These families are just unwilling to incorporate educational recommendations, despite having the ability to do so.

It is important to discern the *true* reasons behind noncompliance. You then need to prioritize the needed home support and work to obtain as much help as possible under the prevailing circumstances. These circumstances should drive your actions, which will need to be creative and flexible as you attempt different approaches to the problem.

A few suggestions that may help families to be more supportive are the following:

- Assign homework that does not need help from a parent or other family member.
- Find someone outside the home but within the home environment (e.g., neighborhood peer, babysitter, church group) who could help.
- Incorporate family activities (e.g., sporting events, household chores, vacation trips, shopping, and entertainment venues) into homework assignments.
- Provide a list of community resources that can help parents support educational recommendations.

9. Parents Who Lack Objectivity

Although we might wish parents could be more objective about their children, such an expectation is unrealistic. All of their hopes and fears are tied up into who their child is, what their child does, and what their child can accomplish. They all want the best for their children, and when you present a problem or a need, their emotions come into play, and their ability to remain objective is compromised.

Fear drives negative emotions. A major source of fear is a lack of control. When parents become difficult, it is often that sense of loss of control and its subsequent fear that drive their actions. Therefore, find ways to give parents control over what you are involving them in and asking them for.

Some suggestions to ease parental fear and negativity are the following:

- Talk about positives first and elicit their views of their child.
- Remain objective yourself (not always easy but certainly easier for you than them).
- Present information and issues in a supportive, understandable manner (do not use jargon).
- Be empathetic with their situation(s).
- Be supportive of their feelings and ideas that are legitimate.
- Be flexible and offer them choices from which to select.
- Be willing to compromise on your requests and demands.

10. Parents Who Have Personal Needs That Get in the Way of Their Child's Needs

Sometimes, the needs of parents or family situations are at odds with the needs of the student. Examples of this can be found in numerous custody orders that clearly are made to be "fair and equitable" to the adults but may, in fact, be counterproductive to the welfare of the child. The arrangement may leave the child with no sense of consistency or control, or the child may be separated from one or more of the significant people in his or her life. While some of these arrangements might be understandable, unavoidable, or impossible to correct, either condition can lead to potential academic and behavioral problems.

Another common condition can be found in homes where children are virtually left to their own devices. In some families, an adult is never or rarely at home when the child is home from school. The reasons for this vary from necessary financial reasons (e.g., parent *has* to work to keep the family housed and fed) to purely personal preferences (e.g., parent travels a lot, goes out a lot).

Unfortunately, when a family goes into crisis mode, the personal needs of the parent or family simply outweigh the educational needs of the child. Often, the home issues (e.g., drugs, alcohol, sexual abuse, extreme poverty, health) completely consume the time and energy of the family. Simple survival is the mode of operation, and education simply cannot compete.

Whatever the reason for the discrepancy between the parent's needs and the child's, the potential for problems to arise in the school-home relationship is increased. Once again, if the discrepancy can be identified, it might be able to be dealt with. Simply pressing the needs of the child onto the parent will not work. Most often, parents are very aware of the problem but are unable or don't know how to fix it.

Added to the list of other suggestions made about getting the family support from community resources, with conditions as described above, it is imperative that you do the following:

- Understand as much of the parameters of the parent's need as possible.
- Try to find ways to work around the family situation.
- Provide information objectively and work with the parent to find a possible solution to the problem.
- Be very empathetic and ready to compromise with a creative solution that will meet the needs of both parent and student.

TEACHER CONDITIONS

Less Likely				More Likely
1	2	3	4	5

1. Teachers Who Have a "We/They" Mentality Toward the Parent, Child, or Home

Often, when things have not gone well, or something has happened that erodes the trust between home and school, teachers will develop a "we/they" attitude toward parents. They do not feel that parents are working with them and think they may even be working against them. When this perception exists, it is understandable and quite normal to be defensive. Unfortunately, this defensiveness only serves to drive words and actions that do nothing but further erode the relationship that is so vital to the student's success.

Once the boundaries are set and it is obvious that there is a we/they attitude in play, it is very difficult to hide our feelings and convince parents that *anything* we ask for or do is for the benefit of their child. It becomes harder to ensure that the student is the central issue.

The old adage "just because you're paranoid doesn't mean they aren't out to get you" may, at times, be true. Your suspicions of their "ill intent" may be true. However, in order to move past the perceived threat and build a stronger, more collaborative relationship, it is important to at least try to hide your suspicions and fears.

Some ways to attenuate this ultimately destructive attitude include the following:

- Meeting with parents and listening carefully to them without using any defensive statements or posture
- Investigating the cause of the parents' actions to determine why we might be feeling like "the enemy"
- Making sure that your suggestions and requests are made with the benefit of the child in mind
- Acknowledging your own insecurities with the situation to determine what you need to do better or differently to garner trust from the family
- Gathering support from other teachers, administrators, or professionals who might help you deal with parental issues

2. Teachers Whose Personal Interests or Convenience Overshadows Student Needs or Compliance

There is no question that the workday of a competent, caring teacher is filled with minute-to-minute activities and necessary tasks. Time constraints are always an issue, and the careful organization of processes and procedures is necessary. Therefore, asking teachers to "go the extra mile" or do something that will take extra time or require a diversion from normal practice can be overwhelming.

The last thing a parent wants to hear is that there is no time for the teacher to meet their child's needs. Another excuse that provokes frustration is being told that what the parent is requesting cannot be done because "precedent will be set" (i.e., union concerns), or since the teacher can't possibly do it for all of the students, they can't do it for one. Likewise, citing "administrative obstacles or policies" interfering with what should be done is a trigger for parents' frustration.

The key idea here is that parents really don't care about precedent, time constraints, policies, or personal interests when it comes to meeting the needs of their child. They have entrusted the care and welfare of their child to the school, and they expect that the child's needs will be met in order for them to learn. They expect that teachers' care will extend beyond the norms, workday, and their own comfort level to accommodate their child's educational needs. While these expectations may not be fair, they are, nevertheless, a reality.

The following are some considerations and proactive measures that will go a long way toward garnering trust and saving time in the long run:

- Setting aside some time before, during, or after the school day to make *quick* phone calls to touch base with parents on issues—positive and negative
- Explaining to parents that you will try to find ways to meet their child's needs without breaking a school rule or policy (shows a willingness to find creative solutions to the problem)
- Identifying those students who may need you to do something extraordinary for them and clearly articulating why you cannot do it for all (e.g., meeting with parents on the weekend)
- Exploring new areas of interest that motivate the student and their family
- Being patient and thoughtfully and truthfully explaining what you can and cannot do and why

3. Teachers Who Give Parents Incorrect Information About Regulations or Administrative Intent

There is nothing more detrimental to the relationship between school and home than for teachers to give parents false or misleading information. This often happens with no ill intent from the teacher. To the contrary, teachers often try hard to give some explanation or information that will answer a parent's questions or allay their fears, only to find out that they have to backtrack later when the full story or correct explanation comes out. For example, citing a scholastic-eligibility policy incorrectly and making a parent believe that his or her child could not participate in a specific sporting event, when, in fact, the policy allows for exceptions to be made. Finding out later that the child could have participated and didn't could erode trust.

It is far better to say nothing or admit that you do not know the complete details than to give incorrect information. That way, you don't lead the parent to believe something that will have to be retraced or into actions that are difficult to repair. Misunderstandings are much harder to resolve than increasing understanding once you have all of the correct information.

Some practical guidelines to help you avoid giving incorrect information include the following:

- Keeping abreast of all education laws and regulations impacting your classroom, school requests, or demands
- Making sure that your rationale for requesting compliance with classroom or school needs is solidly based on accurate and consistent information
- Being open and honest with parents about what information you do and don't know
- Seeking additional information or clarification of administrative intent if unsure
- Setting all assumptions aside before providing parents with information that could be based on false premises

4. Teachers Who Are Rigid With Procedures and Program Flexibility

It is reasonable for teachers to maintain certain program standards and procedures. In fact, there are many procedures that must be followed in order to maintain curriculum and instruction integrity. However, if teachers are overly rigid with those procedures or refuse to adapt or modify their instructional program despite student need, parents will feel that the program matters more than the child. In fact, they will feel very strongly that the individual student is of no concern as long as the program is preserved.

It is not difficult to understand why this situation could lead to parental hard feelings and a lack of trust in the teacher's or school's ability to do what is best for their child. The relationship is undermined, and collaboration between home and school is compromised.

The following are key questions for teachers to consider before refusing to vary their procedures or program:

- Can the student succeed with the current procedural structure?
- Will flexing the program or procedures jeopardize the entire classroom or school?
- Is there sufficient rationale to allow for one or more of the procedures to be modified?
- Are there legal or ethical reasons to remain fixed on the procedures or program?

- Are there legal or ethical reasons to explain a departure from the norm?
- Are there legal or ethical reasons to change procedures for the sake of the child?

5. Teachers Who Lose Objectivity in Student Matters

Anyone who has taught for more than a few years knows that sometimes a particular student can get the best of us. Despite all of our time, efforts, attention, and care, some students just manage to try our patience and leave us feeling defeated and exhausted from all of the effort. When this happens, we lose faith in our ability or our stamina to keep working with the child. Students with significant behavioral needs are among the most common of these challenges.

It is easy to see how a student who drives us to this point can cause us to lose our objectivity. However, once we lose that objectivity, we lose our own credibility and belief in our ability to do what is best for the student. Often, this subjectivity is noticeable to the student, the student's peers, the parents, or all of the above—which erodes authority and makes for negative relationships.

Helpful teacher strategies when struggling with student objectivity include the following:

- Focusing on the issue at hand and asking yourself what you would do if it were related to a different student (preferably one whom you have not had any problems with)
- Asking a colleague how they would handle the situation if it were one of their students
- Stepping back and analyzing the situation from a purely analytical viewpoint
- Acknowledging your feelings outright and setting them aside from the practical, educationally sound manner in which you should be addressing the issue
- Taking deep breaths and considering the needs the child's behavior is demonstrating
- Carefully planning how you will handle a student's challenging behavior and following the plan
- Being accountable to a colleague for following the plan you've developed

6. Teachers Who Assign, Evaluate, or Judge Parental Motivation

Sometimes, it is very difficult to know what motivates parents to ask, say, or execute some of the things they do in the course of a school year. When things are going well, their motivation rarely matters. However, when the relationship is rocky or problems arise, knowing what motivates the parent can often be difficult to ascertain. At those times, an ordinary teacher reaction is often an attempt to assign or judge parental motivation.

This calculation can be useful if the assigned motivation is correct. However, if the teacher is wrong and articulates or acts on the incorrect assumption, major problems can arise that might irreparably damage the school-home relationship. It is important for teachers to do the following:

- Keep your focus on the situation and how to resolve it—not on your assumptions or judgments about what is motivating parents.
- Remain as objective and nonjudgmental as possible or, failing that, work hard to keep your opinions, evaluations, or judgments to yourself.
- Do not discuss with just anyone your opinions or thoughts regarding why parents may be motivated to do what they are doing—seek help from objective sources (e.g., counselor, social worker, administrator).

7. Teachers Who Are Unwilling to Consider Home Information

When the information coming from home is radically different from what is observed and documented in school, it is difficult to take the reported information from home seriously. On the other hand, school and home behavior can be significantly different, and all home documentation should be considered part of the child's total information package.

There are few things that upset parents more than a teacher negating or dismissing information or observations brought from home. Therefore, it is imperative to good working relationships that teachers do the following:

- Seek any and all information that parents share regarding their observations, ideas, or opinions from home.
- Listen carefully to parents' home documentation and probe for details and explanations of circumstances surrounding their observations.

8. Teachers Whose Emotions Cause Them to Take Parental Concerns or Complaints Personally

When someone angrily attacks your personal or professional actions, it is very difficult *not* to take the comments personally. Parents' concerns or complaints have little to do with the teacher personally and instead center on their own educational fears and biases. Or, the specifics of the situation may cause the parent to react negatively.

Once you display a defensive posture, it is difficult to convince parents that you have the child's best interests in mind and have done what is professionally appropriate. Once this defensive posture starts, it becomes harder and harder to resolve the issue and move on. Some tactics that might be helpful (albeit difficult) when a parent expresses a concern or complaint about you or the school include the following:

- Listening carefully to their concerns or complaints, making eye contact, and taking notes as they talk
- Openly asking probing or clarifying questions to get to the rationale behind their concerns or complaints
- Restating their concerns so that both parties know they are understood
- Objectively stating the facts in descriptive terms
- Looking for avenues of agreement and pointing them out
- Weighing their level of concern and looking for compromise if possible

9. Teachers Who Fear a Creative Solution Will Open a Floodgate of Demand

One of the most common fears that teachers express when asked to do something unique or different is that if they do it for one child, they'll have to do it for another. If they find a creative solution to a problem, they will have to find creative solutions for all children. What's "fair" is sameness, and doing something different is "not fair" to the other children.

Nothing upsets families more than to be told that the "rules" or "way things are done" is blocking their child's need. Unions often step in to make sure that teachers don't "set a precedent" and do something that the administration can construe as "past practice" or the norm of "doing business." Teachers are often afraid that if they give extra time or credit or homework variations, for example, they will be asked to do it for all. "I can't individualize for every child" is a common response from teachers who are asked to vary their approaches or take a different tact with a situation.

When faced with the need to find a creative solution to a situation, keep in mind that responsible teaching calls for myriad approaches and solutions to meet the needs of the different children we have in our classrooms. The following suggestions will help you protect your right to decide when and where to divert from the norm and not fall prey to those who insist you can't do something due to the precedent it might set:

- Develop a clear, written rationale for the exception that is made.
- Keep the child first and foremost in the decision.
- Document your actions and their results.

10. Teachers Who Provide Incomplete or Subjective Documentation

One significant cause of difficult school-home relationships is a problem's lack of documentation. Too often teachers and schools expect families to believe what is being reported without documentation or proof. A second significant cause of problems is when the documentation or proof provided is subjective and can be interpreted in different ways.

It is imperative that teachers keep good records of grades and grading systems, keep work samples and tests that illustrate competencies, and maintain good logs of student and parent contacts, especially regarding difficult situations. *Document, document, document* is the key to maintaining good relationships in all situations. The key to this documentation is objectivity. *Be the camera.* Document what is said, done, produced, and witnessed, not what is felt or what tone is used.

These strategies can help with documenting information:

- Keep a spiral notebook to log parental telephone conversations by date and time. (Spiral notebooks document chronology since pages cannot be inserted after the fact.)
- Keep spiral notebooks on individual students to note key conversations, incidents, successes, and problems that arise with the student or parent.
- Maintain a student work folder with samples from all subject areas that illustrate their competencies and difficulties in each subject.

- Provide parents with a folder of your grading, discipline, and homework systems.
- Provide parents with an open invitation to discuss any issues they feel are important to their child's education.

ADMINISTRATOR CONDITIONS

Less Likely				More Likely
1	2	3	4	5

1. Administrators Who Fail to Give Accurate and Ready Feedback to Staff

In an effort to protect teachers, administrators sometimes fail to let them know when parents have raised issues or concerns with their teaching or classroom situations. Sometimes, they get busy and are forced to tell the teacher later. On occasion, they might believe that their own intervention with the parent has diverted the problem, eliminating the need to talk with the teacher. The point is that the teacher is often the last to know that a problem exists.

Parents reported that often "things didn't change" after they talked with the administrator, despite assurances that they would. It is wise to remember that it is never a good idea to assume that a problem will go away on its own or be resolved without all parties actively participating in its resolution.

It is important that administrators directly involve teachers in parental concerns or complaints. The following are some administrator actions that can help avoid this problem:

- Contacting the teacher immediately upon receiving a parent's phone call, even if they don't tell you what the problem is before meeting with you
- Being open with the teacher in a blameless and nonconfrontational manner
- Getting an assessment of a child's academic and behavioral issues through a discussion with the teacher
- Asking the teacher to be "on call" to meet with parents
- Sharing with the parent your need to have the teacher fully involved in the problem's resolution

2. Administrators Who Manage Issues Based on Student Likeability

It is human nature to respond to individuals based on how likeable they are. In a school setting, likeability is often judged by the rate and degree of disciplinary intervention a student causes. The more an administrator has to negatively intercede with a student, the more unlikeable the student may appear to the administrator.

It is of no help that school discipline processes almost always increase the severity of consequences incrementally based on the number of student offenses. Our legal system follows the same principle: the more you get into trouble, the more severe the consequences.

Parents are often angered by an administrator following this process and treating their child harshly because of prior reputation or incidences, rather than analyzing each situation separately and taking it at face value. They reported that their children were not "listened to" or even given a chance to explain their side of the story. Sometimes, there was little to no discussion about the event before a disciplinary action was taken.

No matter how difficult a child is or has been, it is important to convey fairness to the student and the family. While this is not always easy to do, some actions that might help proactively are listed below:

- Make it a point to get to know the difficult students in a nondisciplinary activity.
- Try to develop a relationship with these students outside of the school office.
- Listen carefully to what these students are saying and take notes to refer to later.
- Go out of your way to tell parents the academic and behavioral successes of these students.
- Contact the parents of your "target" students with good news and nondisciplinary issues.

3. Administrators Who Overemphasize the Child's Family History

Students need to be judged and valued for their own merits and behaviors. One of the biggest mistakes an administrator can make is to base his or her reactions or expectations on past experience with the student's family. The student may be achieving at a lower level than other family members who have gone through the school, causing the administrator disappointment or frustration. This can cause overreactions that result in interactions or decisions that are based on that frustration.

Alternately, a student may be achieving at a higher level or may be much more of a model student than his or her other family members. If the administrator expects less due to past experience with the family, the student will be undervalued from the start, and reactions or decisions might be filled with unwarranted skepticism.

While it is only natural to compare students or reflect on past experiences with a student's family, it is imperative that administrators strive to deal with each student individually, without prior prejudices. The following suggestions can help in this endeavor:

- Avoid comparing students to their other family members (e.g., "you're just like your brother").
- Get to know students personally so that you don't underestimate or overestimate their abilities.
- Be careful not to reference other family traits or incidences that were problematic when dealing with students or their parents.

4. Administrators Who Fail to Provide Staff Development

One of the biggest mistakes administrators make is to assume that teachers can handle any and all situations presented to them without formal discussion, training, or staff development. Far too often, administrators wait until after a situation or crisis occurs to act, and providing appropriate support after the fact is seldom easy.

Education professionals need a variety of staff development opportunities to deal with the wide range of cultures, family situations, and educational issues they face on a daily basis. In addition to staff development on curriculum and instruction, addressing personal growth, conflict resolution strategies, interpersonal styles, communication strategies, and anger management can be very beneficial to educators and have a positive impact on the school environment.

Of particular importance to staff development programs is the arsenal of skills teachers and administrators must have to understand and develop strategies for the following:

- Personalities and learning differences
- Working with culturally diverse students and families
- Poverty and its effects on learning
- Useful behavioral interventions for the disruptive or behaviorally challenging student
- Motivational and instructional strategies to promote active participation of all students
- Differentiated instruction for diverse learners in the same classroom
- Grading and homework strategies to meet the needs of diverse learners
- Inclusive practices

5. Administrators Who Overuse Professional Jargon When Communicating With Parents

Education is full of professional jargon that is used to quickly share information. While educators know and understand what *NCLB, IOWA Tests, AYP,* and *benchmarks* mean, most parents do not. Yet we often use these terms and assume parents understand what is being discussed.

The use of jargon works very well to frustrate and anger parents. They may sit and nod (no one likes to look ignorant), but if they are made to feel lost or insecure, it is almost guaranteed to put obstacles between school and home. It is like being invited to a party where no one speaks your language! Avoiding jargon and using simple terminology as much as possible will help ensure that parents can participate fully in the educational process, particularly with a problem or when an explanation of a difficult situation is needed.

Administrators need to talk with parents in simple, clearly stated terms. To avoid communication obstacles, keep the following strategies in mind:

- Use full terms instead of acronyms: for example, *No Child Left Behind* instead of *NCLB.*
- Explain terminology in a short, precise manner.
- Provide definitions of frequently used acronyms prior to discussing them.
- Openly acknowledge that a lot of educational jargon is used and ask up front if anything needs to be explained or reviewed before the discussion ends.
- Direct the parent to signal you when you've used a term that they don't understand.

6. Administrators Who Give Inadequate Responses to Parents' Concerns, Questions, or Requests

It is imperative that administrators respond to a parent's communication as soon as possible. The administrator will often want to investigate an issue with the teacher before calling or seeing the parent. However, the more responsive an administrator is (i.e., the faster and more "up front" the response time), the more valued the parent will feel.

The following actions will help prevent obstacles in the school-home relationship:

- Take phone calls whenever physically possible to do so.
- Return phone messages as soon as possible, especially those you may not want to.
- Make appointments to meet with parents in person as soon as feasible for both parties.
- Listen calmly with no interruptions until the parent is finished.
- Take notes while the parent is talking.
- Explain clearly what your next step will be before answering their request and make sure you follow through.
- Make sure that the information you give in the initial meeting or follow-up conversations is truthful, accurate, and as complete as possible.

7. Administrators Who Fail to Ask Up Front for a Desired Solution to a Parent's Issue

When a parent raises an objection to something the school has done or will be doing, it is normal to be on the defensive. However, if administrators view the objections as opportunities rather than obstacles, parental involvement might serve well to improve educational practices. Asking parents up front what they desire is a great way to clearly delineate the desired solution and determine if it can or should be accomplished. If it's not feasible, a further discussion of the situation is warranted to help both parties understand the "why not" of the proposed solution.

Navigating around this roadblock can also bring both parties to an even better solution that will serve both parties well. In order to find a resolution to a problematic situation, try the following:

- Ask early on what the parent would like to happen.
- Be ready to offer more than one resolution that is amenable to the school.
- Make sure that your explanations are accurate and logical.
- Be open to a parent's suggestions and compromises.

8. Administrators Who Fail to Document the Chronology of Prior Interventions, Obstacles, or Remediations Used With the Child or Home

One way to avoid significant problems between home and school is to keep careful documentation of school efforts to work with the family, help the child, and establish a good school-home connection. One obstacle that was reported frequently by parents and teachers was a lack of documentation of the many efforts made by home and school to make things work effectively and smoothly. It is important to note dates and times when documenting.

Parents need to know the many actions taken on behalf of their child before a situation becomes a problem. A single incident rarely reaches the level where home and school are at odds unless there has been little to no communication and cooperation between them. Making sure efforts to work and clearly communicate with the home are documented offers support for an institutional history of issues.

Key strategies to document school efforts include the following:

- Maintaining spiral notebooks on those students that are "red flagged" for potentially contentious school-home issues
- Keeping telephone logs of all calls to and from the home with date, time, purpose of call, key items discussed, and parental responses in quotes
- Maintaining student folders with both problematic issues and successes and strengths that can be shared with the parent

9. Administrators Who Are Overly Rigid With Procedures and Programs

Just as with teachers, parents need to feel that administrators see their children as individuals with specialized needs and considerations. One of the most discussed and intensely emotional red flags raised by parents was that of the administrator who does not see the children, only the "rules." While it is necessary and important for administrators to maintain order and follow the rules, it is equally important and necessary for those same administrators to flex where possible to accommodate the child's needs and understand the unique circumstances surrounding the situation at hand.

Keeping the established procedures and rules in mind, administrators would be wise to consider the following:

- Thoroughly investigate the circumstances surrounding the situation, event, or request.
- Analyze and understand the academic and emotional needs of the student.
- Listen carefully to the information shared by teachers, parents, or other school personnel.
- Consider alternative solutions to meet the needs of the child without sacrificing the integrity of the rules or procedures.

10. Administrators Who View Objections as Obstacles, Not Opportunities

Education is under attack from many venues, and with so much public criticism of our schools today, it is difficult for administrators to not react defensively. However, if parent and family objections are weighed carefully (individually and collectively), administrators can accomplish two things. First, they will establish a stronger school-home connection by being viewed as responsive and caring. Second, they can gain valuable information about what is working or lacking in their school.

Many of our best ideas and school improvements come from a parent's perspective or reaction to a situation. Some of those come from parental objections or skepticism to something we have said, done, or proposed. Parents at odds with the school will naturally feel disenfranchised. Several ways to attenuate that feeling among parents in your school community include the following:

- Viewing objections and concerns as opportunities to make improvements or adjustments
- Openly asking parents to voice their concerns about things happening in the school, their child's classroom, or with the administration

- Keeping a written list of parental concerns and actions taken to address them
- Carefully investigating and analyzing the individual and collective concerns raised
- Sharing your investigation and analysis, along with possible solutions, with staff and parents
- Acknowledging errors and mistakes

SUMMARY

A six-month study involving surveys, interviews, and listening sessions with parents, teachers, and administrators in separate venues afforded us an opportunity to collect data about relationships between home and school. These data then gave us a chance to look carefully at some common themes that arose from specific parent or family, teacher, and administrator conditions that gave rise to positive and negative feelings and experiences. In fact, it appears that the stronger the existence of an identified condition, the more likely it was that a negative relationship existed between home and school. Conversely, it was found that the weaker the existence of the condition, the more likely it was that a positive relationship existed.

Recognizing the primary hazards to school-home relationships is a means to adopting key proactive strategies. Several strategies and suggestions to help attenuate or eradicate the impact of the specific conditions have been identified for consideration, trial, or adaptation. The following additional, more "global" strategies are offered to help with determining the existence of any of the common conditions identified above and to assist you in your efforts to build more positive partnerships:

- Keep a log of parental issues and concerns raised and any actions taken to address them.
- Carefully investigate and analyze individual and collective issues and concerns raised to look for underlying causes or commonalities.
- Focus on the individual student's needs and those of the family.
- Develop and implement strategies to address the individual and collective issues interfering with positive school-home relationships.

Honing Solid Communication Skills

Communication is the most important asset to a good working relationship.

—Fran Lee, Kansas State Department of Education

The key to any relationship is strong, positive communication between the two parties. Educators must hone their communication skills and present themselves as open, warm, and welcoming to parents. While most of us are very aware of what constitutes appropriate verbal and nonverbal behavior, it is often difficult to practice in the midst of challenging situations—especially with those individuals who we find difficult to communicate with.

We communicate in many different ways. Our words, tone, body language, the physical space we place between those we are communicating with, and our facial expressions speak clearly to others. Even our silence and lack of body language can speak volumes.

We all recognize, for the most part, that misunderstandings, misinformation, and disagreements can put a wall up between communicating parties. But there are some very common communicative behaviors than can do the same thing. Parents in our study were very articulate in identifying verbal and nonverbal teacher or administrator behaviors that caused them to feel uncomfortable, angry, or downright hostile toward the teacher or the school.

We will discuss some of the verbal and nonverbal obstacles cited by parents as reasons why they felt their relationship with the school was less than they would have desired. In our summary, we list suggested proactive measures for your consideration, and suggest you add your own thoughts and ideas.

VERBAL COMMUNICATION OBSTACLES

Directive Statements

Statements that start with "You must" or "You will have to" almost always trigger a defensive response. Yet educators tend to use these types of statements frequently because we are professionally trained to know how to help schoolchildren. The intent is positive, but the reaction is most often negative. It is never wise to tell a parent what they must do using direct statements like those above. Doing so tends to put them into a defensive mode and can lead to anger or alienation. After all, these are *their* children, and they feel that they know them best. They may think we have intruded on their role as parents.

At the beginning of the year, a middle school music department sent home parent notification of the "contract rules" that were to be followed by students participating in choir or band. Stated, quite emphatically, was a list of things that students and parents *must* do. For example, rule number one demanded that "students must practice for a half hour each day or risk being removed from band." Furthermore, it stated that if a student or parent failed to comply with *any* of the rules, the student would not be allowed to remain in the activity.

We're sure you can guess what the reaction was! While the intentions were good, and the list of *musts* was meant to ensure the students' success, the directness and tone were not appreciated and did not garner positive feelings with many parents. Consider how the reaction to the rules might have been different (i.e., positive) if they had been worded more "indirectly" (e.g., "At least a half hour of practice per day is strongly suggested to ensure the student's increased skill level and continued participation in band").

Threatening Statements

Statements that start with "If you don't do this, then" trigger negative responses of significant magnitude, especially if parents don't agree with what you are telling them to do. Yet, as we know, we are often faced with having to explain the consequences of not following through on a school rule or procedure, which can often sound like a threat.

Disciplinary and child health and safety issues are always problematic, especially when parents have not followed through on procedural or legal obligations. Any secondary teacher or administrator who has been involved in a formal hearing regarding a student's possible suspension knows how tense the communications can be and how easy it would be to threaten severe consequences if compliance is not forthcoming.

While it is necessary for us to lay out the laws, policies, and procedures that must be followed, it's *how* we impart the information that is critical to the relationship. Instead of using the pronoun *you*, take the person out of the mix and simply make factual statements about what would happen if an action doesn't occur. For example, instead of saying to the parent, "If you don't make sure that John's attendance improves, he will not be allowed to take the final exam and will not pass the course," you could simply state that "District policy will not allow John to take the final exam if he misses more than *X* classes."

Preaching Statements

Parent after parent has reacted negatively when they have been told what they "should do" or what their "responsibility to do" was. They know and understand what is needed to be done and don't like to feel as though they are ignorant and need to be told what to do. For example, being tardy is often a problem with students, particularly at the secondary level. Parents understand that their student needs to get to school on time. Simply saying, "I know you recognize the importance of being in school at the first bell, and Sam needs to get here on time, so how can we help you make that happen?" is one strategy.

One case in point involved a young boy who was presenting significant behavioral and academic issues at school. In talking with him, it became clear that he was going to bed very late, watching TV during the night, and getting very little sleep. When contacted, his mother acknowledged that she knew he was not getting enough sleep but just couldn't get him to go to bed and certainly couldn't "stay up all night to make sure he stayed in bed." Our immediate thought was, "You're the mother, and it's your responsibility to make sure he sleeps." Instead, we sat down with her and brainstormed some ideas on how we might be able to help her with this issue. Together, we came up with a home behavior plan and a reward-based follow-up at school. In a short time, the plan worked, and the boy's behavior and academics improved.

Advising Statements

Our parents reported that nothing has angered them more than being told, "What I would do is this." It made them feel inferior, even when the parent asked what the educator would do! Adding the phrase "I can offer some advice, but keep in mind this is unique to you and your family" before making an advising statement recognizes that you naturally can't know everything about the situation.

If we had a dime for every time parents said, "You don't know what you would do because you don't have a child or situation like mine," we'd be rich. They are right. Even if you have *similar* circumstances, they are not completely alike. So limit your advice to suggestions, ideas, and possible actions that might be considered, and don't make the parent feel as though if it were you, the solution would be obvious. It comes across as arrogant.

Judging Statements

Several parents reported school staff making explicit judgments about their family or parenting skills. "You're not thinking straight," "You need to be home more," and "You need to take more time with your son" were examples given. These are roadblocks to any kind of positive relationship, regardless of the truth.

Homework often arises as an issue on which teachers judge parents. When students don't do their homework, we may blame this on parents' unwillingness or inability to help their child complete the assignment. Rather than making judgments that may be ill-informed, we need to elicit information to understand the situation and then address the circumstances preventing the homework from being completed. Adjusting our attitude and approach is more likely to help ensure that the students get the work done.

Excusing Statements

No matter what your opinion of a parent's concern, avoid making light of his or her fears, anxieties, or objections. Saying "It's not so bad" or "It's not a problem" has the opposite effect of what is intended. Parents stated that these kinds of statements demonstrate the school's "lack of understanding of the problem," and they fear the situation must get much worse before the school will intervene.

In one particular situation involving transportation, a group of parents were highly agitated that their children were "losing instructional time" because they were leaving their classrooms five minutes early each day to board their buses. The parents were told by the building administrator that it wasn't a problem because it was only five minutes. They asked for a meeting at our district office and expressed their concerns about the time lost and their impression that the school didn't care about their children.

Upon investigation, we discovered that those particular buses carried students who lived farther away and were moved to the front of the bus queue so those children would not arrive home much later than their classmates. We brainstormed some ideas on how to rearrange the buses' arrival times and still ensure that classroom instructional time wasn't lost. This resolution eased the tensions that had developed.

Prying Statements

Far too often, in our quest to get all the information we can to resolve an issue, we go too far and pry into family matters. Parents reported being outraged at being asked "What haven't you told us?" or hearing the words "There must be more that you are unwilling to tell us." Keep your questioning gentle and be understanding of their need for privacy, even if added information might impact the situation.

Health and safety are areas where we often need to take more assertive action when gathering information. Yet it is precisely these two areas that families feel are most private. It is our obligation to explain to parents why we need the information we do and how that information can help us to best meet their child's needs.

In one situation, parents cut off all communication with the school nurse because of statements she made after finding out some crucial medical information about their daughter. The young girl was a diabetic, and the parents had not reported that to the school. Consequently, when the girl had a minor low-blood-sugar incident, the nurse was not able to quickly correct the situation. It was only after the girl told her she "needed some sugar" that the nurse started to guess what was going on. She called the parents and asked directly if the girl was a diabetic, and the mother confirmed it. The nurse then said, "You put your daughter in jeopardy. I want to know everything about her health!" The mother hung up and did not communicate directly with the nurse after that, which was obviously problematic from time to time. Had the nurse conveyed the same need in a different manner, such as by saying, "Knowing your daughter's health issues allows us to plan ahead and respond to any health-related situations quickly and efficiently," the lines of communication might have remained open.

Sarcastic Statements

When frustrated, we often resort to sarcasm to express the irony of the situation we find ourselves in. For some, it is a form of humor that expresses our frustration. Said sarcastically, "Good luck" or "Won't happen in this lifetime" are highly discouraging to parents. Sarcasm has no place in a discussion with parents concerned about their child or a school situation. By definition, sarcasm is used to cut or inflict pain—not something we ever want to do.

Teachers and administrators need to be careful when saying no to something a parent wants for his or her child. Often, the request may be something that we agree needs to happen. For example, parents may request a change in classroom assignment, but the administration has a policy against such requests. The teacher might even be as frustrated as the parents with the child's assignment. Consequently, our sarcasm rises to the surface. Or, we may think that if we dismiss the parent's request with a cynical remark (e.g., "Administration *never* does that"), they will drop it. While we assume we may be making allies of the parents, we are actually pitting them against the school system and, since we are a part of that system, ourselves.

Avoidance Statements

It's normal to want to avoid problems and confrontations. However, making statements to concerned parents such as "Let's not talk about this now" or "I don't have time for this" serves only to heighten their anxiety and often increases their anger. Instead, express your mutual concern and desire to resolve the issue, setting a time as soon as possible, if not then, to fully discuss the parent's issue.

Sometimes, parents need some time to cool down and reflect on their concerns. It is difficult to talk rationally in the heat of anger. One strategy that works well is to tell parents you want to give them your full attention, so you need to set up a time to talk specifically about their issue. You should, however, listen to enough information up front to make sure that the issue is not urgent and can actually wait to be discussed.

Diagnostic Statements

As educators, our job description includes diagnosing and remediating student learning and behavioral issues. That's where it ends. Parents have reported being told "Your problem is" and "Home is the problem" when teachers had reached the conclusion that the school had done all it could. What parents heard was that they were on their own and that only if things changed at home would things get better at school. This is extremely discouraging to those parents and families who could not, would not, or perhaps even *should* not change anything at home. Placing the blame on the home situation has an extremely detrimental effect on the relationship.

As professional educators, we are accustomed to assessing and diagnosing situations and finding solutions to obstacles or problems. While we may be highly skilled at this as a result of extensive experience, we need to tread very carefully when it comes to diagnosing issues we believe are caused by home situations.

Any good diagnosis relies on the amount and veracity of the information provided. How do we ever know if we have all of the information we need from home or if the information we have is accurate?

NONVERBAL COMMUNICATION OBSTACLES

Eye Movements

Eye contact is an important regulator of communication. Interest in the topic, speaker, or audience is often conveyed by eye contact. The number one offensive eye movement parents report is rolling the eyes when there is disagreement, disinterest, or frustration. Usually it signals exasperation but is often interpreted as contempt or condescension. Rolling your eyes is lethal to the meeting and often to the future relationship between home and school. Other negative eye behaviors identified by parents as being rude or frustrating were staring, looking away when eye contact is made, lack of eye contact altogether, peering over glasses, and raising one eyebrow.

One particularly memorable meeting brought this lesson home to all of us fortunate enough to be present. I say *fortunate* because every once in a while a learning opportunity comes from adversity. At this meeting, a particularly combative parent was demanding several things from her son's educational team that were, in all honesty, a bit far-fetched and, in our opinion, unwarranted. One of the team members was rolling her eyes each time the parent spoke. Before I could quietly signal that staff member to stop, the mother jumped up and screamed, "I'm sick and tired of you rolling your eyes every time I say something. Who do you think you are?" She then turned and stormed out. The meeting was officially ended, but we sat as a team and discussed eye rolling and how destructive it is to the communication process. Appropriate apologies were made to the parent, and we moved on from there at our rescheduled meeting.

Gestures

Gestures are very helpful when they convey interest and involvement in the topic. However, they can be detrimental to the communication when and if the receiver feels threatened or dismissed. The most common threatening or frustrating gestures cited by parents are the following:

clenched fists, finger-pointing, drumming fingers, and tapping a pencil on the table. We need to be especially diligent with our gestures when we are upset or frustrated with the situation or individual we are talking with.

My own identified stress habit was to tap my pen or pencil on the table. As my emotions rise, my tapping gets faster and harder. My staff noticed this, and on one occasion a member of our legal support team reached over and removed the pen from my hand! He later explained that it was disruptive to his thought process and, essentially, a way of "shouting" at the person speaking or the information shared. He also made me acutely aware that others probably had the same reaction as he did.

Posture

Our posture communicates numerous messages. In our face-to-face meetings with parents and families, how we sit conveys our feelings. Our posture communicates interest in the individuals we are talking with as much as it does our interest in the topic under discussion. Parents reported reacting very negatively to teachers and administrators who slouch, lean backward in their chairs, or cross their arms and legs. Slouching conveys an "I couldn't care less" attitude. Leaning backward conveys an "I want to be out of here" attitude, and crossing the arms and legs conveys a "Say whatever you want, but I'm not changing my mind" attitude. These postures need to be avoided. Replace them, instead, with leaning forward, sitting upright and composed, and maintaining open arms.

Posture conveys attitude. It signals our mind-set and often gives away our feelings toward what is happening or being discussed. It often contradicts the words we are using and rarely goes unnoticed. Make sure that your posture conveys a professional attitude that signals interest, compassion, commitment, and assurance that you have ownership in what is being conveyed.

Physical Distance

Proximity to the listener is critical to the listener's comfort level. Cultural norms dictate this, and we need to respect the norms of the various cultures we are working with. Invading one's space will cause discomfort and exceeding one's space can suggest disinterest. The common proximity issues identified as highly negative by our parents involved distance at a table.

Parents told us that teachers and administrators who sat in larger, higher-level, or more formal-looking chairs and those who sat at the far end of the table (a common practice) or who actually pushed their chair away from the table tended to fuel parents' negative, sometimes angry, feelings. Round or square tables with equidistant seating, on the other hand, were reported as friendlier than long, rectangular ones. Seating that places everyone at similar eye levels is helpful.

Pushing away from the table should be avoided. Parents clearly noticed staff members who sat far from the table or actually moved farther away from the table once the meeting started. Therefore, if there is a need for someone to sit farther away (e.g., a physical condition necessitates it, the person must leave promptly and doesn't want to disrupt the dialogue), note it and briefly explain why it is necessary. The explanation will remove any assumptions the parent might make about the distance between them.

We had one parent who refused to meet with us if one of our service providers was going to be in attendance. Upon prodding, the mother admitted that she did not like this particular staff person because every time she met with her, the staff member would turn her chair away from the mother and make little eye contact throughout their conversations. I asked the staff member about this, and she admitted that it was true, but it was because she was deaf in one ear and needed to put her "good ear" toward the mother when the mother was speaking. Once I explained this to the mother, the problem of the staff member's attendance at our meetings disappeared.

We took deliberate care in the design of a conference room that often hosted difficult meetings. Superintendent's disciplinary hearings, Committee on Special Education meetings, and Board of Education meetings were held in this room. In our efforts to minimize the physical distance issue, we exchanged a very long, rectangular table for a large round one. We replaced stiff, hard-backed chairs with soft, swivel chairs. Both allowed equal physical distance and interactive communication. It seemed to tone down the negativity, even though the information exchanged was the same. Participants almost always remarked about the "friendly" atmosphere of the room—even our own staff!

Head Movements

How we hold and move our heads during a conversation speaks volumes about how we feel about what is being said. Everyone knows that a nod conveys agreement and that the speed or intensity at which we bob our heads conveys the depth of our agreement. We also recognize that shaking our head back and forth connotes disagreement.

Parents identified specific head movements as problematic. Those cited as occurring frequently in conversations with school personnel were head shaking side to side, cocking the head to one side, and lowering the head downward to look at their lap, the table, or floor. When asked what those actions conveyed to them, parents said that all three basically said, "That's not right," "I think you're lying," "I don't believe this," "I don't care," or "I give up." Their obvious reaction to these behaviors was anger and frustration. We need to be aware of our head movements, particularly when the information under discussion is difficult, conflicting, or frustrating.

Facial Expressions

The face is the basic nonverbal mode of communication. What we do with our face conveys our emotions and generally demonstrates to others our friendliness and trustworthiness. Smiles can convey powerful signals of happiness, affiliation, warmth, and empathy.

Parents reported several negative facial expressions that interfered with the feelings they had toward the person exhibiting those expressions. They talked specifically about seeing frowns, clenched teeth, curled lips, and open mouths (surprise) displayed by teachers, particularly when they were expressing concerns or objections. Furthermore, they reported that each of these presented an obstacle to the communication process. Most important, parents identified these negative facial expressions as a major identifier of staff they didn't like, trust, or consider as caring toward their child.

Voice Qualities

Tone, pitch, rhythm, volume, rate of speech, and inflection all communicate our feelings and interest. We need to keep in mind that situational stress can easily alter our voice quality and that we may need to modulate it to maintain positive communication in relationships.

Voice qualities at the top of parents' lists of communication obstacles are high pitch, fast rate with no stops, monotone, and high volume. Tenseness, helplessness, and nervousness are perceived when voice pitch is raised. Educators who speak rapidly with no stops made parents feel controlled and spoken *at* rather than *with*. Speakers who raised their volume and were received as "loud" were perceived as aggressive or overbearing. Those with monotones were perceived as "disinterested" or "rehearsed."

Some of the vocal qualities listed as obstacles above are actual vocal problems some individuals have. Keeping this in mind, if there is a physical issue causing one of these qualities (e.g., high volume due to hearing loss), make sure that you take the time to quickly explain this to parents.

Environment

Communication of meaningful, important, or difficult topics can be facilitated or blocked by the environment in which it takes place. Educators are very busy people, and many of our communications occur "on the run" or whenever or wherever we can "catch" the person we need to talk with. Even many of our formal meetings take place in quickly procured spaces within classrooms or buildings.

Many times, the surroundings in which we meet with parents are meager and uncomfortable. Parents consistently reported meeting with staff in rooms that were "too hot," "too small," or "too cluttered." They sometimes felt like they were "under interrogation" with harsh lighting and stiff furnishings. They reported feeling "trapped" in rooms with no windows and only one way out. Furniture barriers between them and the speaker (e.g., desks, very large tables) increased their anxiety and feelings of being spoken "down to" or "at" rather than "with." Being proactive and avoiding these kinds of environmental obstacles is wise.

Take the time to "warm up" the environment in which you choose to meet with parents. Plants, tablecloths, refreshments on the table, and neat and organized rooms speak loudly to your willingness to bring effort, care, and organization to your job. In turn, this translates to a more comfortable and trusting listener.

SUMMARY

Communication skills and relationships are inseparably connected. The more positive our communication skills, the more positive the relationship can become. In our experience with, and direct questioning of, parents, we were able to identify the key verbal and nonverbal communication obstacles to positive relationships between home and school.

There are many proactive measures you can take to facilitate positive communications. It is especially important that positive measures be taken when there is disagreement, conflict, or negativity involved between home and school. Some key proactive suggestions are as follows:

- Whenever possible, meet in person rather than talking on the phone or writing a note.
- Check periodically for understanding, questions, or feedback from the parent.

- Be sure to make the physical environment of the classroom, meeting room, and school inviting and comfortable for parents.
- Choose your words carefully, especially when there is any negativity in the discussion.
- Keep your negative emotions in check and try not to get sarcastic or dismissive. Patience, kindness, and respect in your communicative approach will go a long way toward preserving the relationship.
- If possible, ask others to observe your nonverbal behavior in meetings and let you know later if you exhibit any of the key communication obstacles identified in this chapter.
- If you notice communication obstacles, do whatever you can to stop them. You might need to call a quick recess (to address the individual(s) directly), or you might need to bring the behavior out into the open to clarify what the problem is (*very* hard to do but effective if done smoothly).

Adopting Key Rules

Everyday life is made more pleasant, saner, and more healthful by the practice of the rules of civility.

—P. M. Forni

As we grow from childhood to adolescence and then adulthood, we learn that specific actions or nonactions can determine the outcomes of our endeavors. Through good and bad experiences, we learn to follow basic "rules of thumb" to enhance our relationships. Relationships with parents of the children we teach are no different. During our work over many years, through discussions and direct experiences, we have honed and come to rely on a set of rules that, if followed, will definitely facilitate positive relationships between home and school.

RULE 1: BE RESPECTFUL

Schools are microcosms of society. All of the problems and issues facing us today exist in the homes of our children. You need to be mindful of the thousands of possible circumstances that could be impacting the family and respectful of the everyday struggles that might be consuming their lives.

We should not be prying into the personal business of a family. Unless we are told of a health or safety issue, or there is a situation interfering with the child's education, we need to respect the family's privacy. Parents deserve to be treated with consideration and deference. We need to lead with empathy and understanding when issues come to light. We might not like or agree with conditions in the home, but it's not our place to judge (unless the child's health or welfare is at risk).

Place value on any and all contributions the family can make to the school and classroom. Accept what is offered if you can, and work to let parents know that you appreciate whatever they can give by way of time, information, assistance in the classroom or at home, or simply their responses to notes or questionnaires sent home.

As an administrator, I was constantly amazed at how teachers would radically change their attitudes and demeanor around parents once they knew the specifics of conditions at home. Their anger would turn to sympathy; their frustrations to acceptance. One memorable example was a team of teachers who wanted a young man suspended for sleeping in class, not paying attention, and not doing homework. When I investigated the situation with the young man and then his mother, I discovered that he was living in a one-room apartment with a new baby sister who had colic and whose crying was keeping him and his mother up all night. He was even walking with the baby throughout the night to calm her. Once the staff knew all of this, they became more tolerant of the boy's fatigue, and time was allotted in school to complete homework.

RULE 2: BE PROACTIVE

There are essentially two ways to approach problems and issues. One approach is to be proactive and try to identify potential issues *before* they become problems. The other approach is to function as a "maintenance" person and react to situations when they arise, solve problems that actually become obstacles, and wait until you have no choice but to address the issue at hand.

Nothing is more important than taking proactive steps to forge positive relationships with parents. Don't wait until a problem arises to take the time to get to know them, interact with them, or provide them with information about yourself, your goals for their children, or your beliefs. The more information shared and the more you interact with parents, the easier it is to forge a relationship and deal with problems and issues when they do arise.

We strongly recommend that you don't choose to be a maintenance person. The problem with this approach is that you are in danger of missing the warning signs of impending problems. By the time your attention is focused on the problem, it might have become larger than if it had been foreseen or proactively avoided.

Proactive measures that work with one family may not work with the next. However, there are some proactive measures that tend to work in all situations. Most educators know the importance of sending good reports home or making positive phone calls to tell parents what their child is doing well—and not waiting until there is a problem to make contact. You know to begin parent conferences with the child's strengths.

What we want to talk about is how to set the scene proactively when you have to deal with a difficult situation or problem. Parental meetings are always tricky. They are usually time-constrained, making it difficult to do much more than review concerns that need to be addressed. Make the time to quickly list the child's positive attributes at the start. It won't take long and will go a long way toward setting a receptive climate for discussion of problems or concerns. Sometimes, it is very hard to find the strengths in a child with many academic and social difficulties. All children have positive qualities. Some may be harder to find than others. Search for them and start there. As one of our most insightful mentors told us, "*Every* child shines at something. It is your job to recognize that area of strength, support and encourage its further development, and then improve weaknesses." By starting with the positives, parents are more likely to accept what might be viewed negatively or difficult to acknowledge.

At the very least, as we have previously discussed, you need to set a warm climate for meetings with parents. In our district, we made a conscious effort to have our meetings at a table that had a tablecloth, flowers, a pitcher of ice water and glasses, and sometimes cookies. Coffee, if possible, is a welcome added touch. All of this may sound trite, but parents reported over and over that they felt "at home" talking with teachers, regardless of the information shared, and parent attendance and participation in the meetings rose dramatically.

Make sure that in addition to the problems and concerns you bring up, you have possible solutions and answers on how to deal with them. Providing multiple options for addressing the issues offers parents some choice, and thereby some control, over the resolution. It goes a long way toward empowering the parent in the educational process and truly making them a partner in their child's education. Additionally, it demonstrates that you have taken the time to seek out and offer possible solutions to help them.

Finally, be proactive in how you gather and disseminate information about a child. The teacher's room is never a place to discuss family dynamics. Never compare siblings or talk about other family members. An overheard conversation often gets reported to others and can get back to the family. Once that happens, it will make future trust-building attempts impossible and can destroy any trust already built with that family or others who hear of the situation.

RULE 3: NO SURPRISES

No one likes to be taken by surprise, especially if the information being shared is of a negative or serious nature. It can become even more problematic if the surprise is potentially damaging to self-esteem or stature.

All stakeholders need to be treated respectfully by being given as much of the available information surrounding an issue as possible. Most importantly, information needs to be shared in a way that respects the emotions, situations, and personal integrity of the individuals involved. Parents should not walk into a meeting with no idea of who will be there, what will be discussed, or what their role will be. It's just as important for teachers to know the meeting's topic.

For that reason, establishing a "no surprises" rule within a school setting is crucial to the establishment of trust between home and school.

- Give parents a "heads-up" when school issues arise that might become problematic down the road.
- Provide a synopsis of meeting topics prior to the actual meeting.
- Investigate situations fully, speaking with all concerned parties before reporting to parents.
- Call parents in advance of meetings to obtain information or allow them to gather background information that might be significant.

If we expect parents to be partners in their child's education, then we have to behave like a partner. We can't surprise them or make them feel ill at ease and then expect them to respond positively or objectively about what we communicate.

Nothing undermines a relationship faster than one person catching another off guard or placing them in a compromised position. In our work over the years, there were many times that staff or parents were taken by surprise and left in a terribly uncomfortable or embarrassing situation. Examples include parent conferences where parents were first told of their child's failure in one or more subjects, end-of-year report cards where "retention recommended" was written without having been brought up with parents before, and formal committee meetings where staff recommended expensive equipment or additional staffing without prior discussion with administration. It is understandable how trust was broken and relationships suffered as a result of these types of incidences.

An altogether too frequent and exemplary surprise to parents is end-of-year recommendations for retention. We have seen numerous cases where, even though it could be argued that the parent "should have" known a child might need to be retained, they didn't. You need to discuss this possibility as soon as you realize that the child may not have enough time to make up lost ground or acquire the skills needed to move on. Your retention and promotion policy should be discussed with the parent well in advance of the end of the school year, and efforts to remediate the situation should be taken with the parent's involvement. It's entirely understandable that parents become very angry when retention is thrown at them at the end of the year.

RULE 4: 24 HOURS

Education is scheduled to the minute, with little time for reflection or quiet deliberation on what needs to be done next. These time constraints make it very hard to stop what is happening and deal with unexpected contacts made by parents—particularly when parents are upset or have an issue they want to discuss.

One way to show respect for parents' concerns and interest in school-related issues, and to convey your desire to have them involved, is to make sure that when they contact the school, that contact is answered no more than 24 hours after it is made. While this rule may be easy to believe in, it is not as easy to practice. Yet it is critical. Often, the time taken to initially make this contact will save you a lot of time and headaches down the road.

Now that most parents have voice mail or e-mail, contact can be made more easily. Even if you don't have the time to talk, make the contact and set a time to talk when you are free to devote your full attention. Make the contact yourself, even if you have to make a call at night or over a weekend, and explain that you don't have the time right now to give your full attention to the matter but are willing to set a day and time for the discussion. We can't expect parents to be involved and then not give them our time and full attention as soon as possible when they make an overture.

An easy method to ensure that you keep this rule is to have a spiral notebook next to your phone to record all phone calls made and received throughout your busy day. Carefully log the date and time of each incoming and outgoing call made and write a short synopsis of the call's content. Note what was said to whom and make sure that you note voice mail details. This becomes invaluable in tracking the response time of your calls.

We have found this rule sometimes difficult to keep. However, with commitment to its purpose and a little ingenuity, getting back to parents quickly can be accomplished. One time, when it was "impossible" for the parent to talk on the phone or meet with us during the day, we offered to meet at "any time that was convenient" for the parent. The meeting took place at 6:30 a.m. and yielded information about this single dad and the home situation. The information not only explained a lot of things that were happening at school but allowed us to work out some solutions and gave the father the information he needed to support our efforts at home.

In another instance, my secretary told me that a student's mother had called and was particularly upset with my office. She wanted a phone call "immediately." I cleared some time and called her within the hour. Most interestingly, she voiced her "shock" that I actually called her back! In addition, she was "amazed" that I returned her call so quickly, especially since she was "loud and angry and not polite" with my secretary. I laughed and told her that if we had done something wrong, I definitely needed to talk to her as quickly as possible. From that point on, the conversation was direct but cordial, and we resolved the issue at hand. More importantly, that parent's stated trust in our office was restored.

RULE 5: NO DUMP TRUCKS ALLOWED

Due to the nature of teaching, allotted time for meetings is usually minimized for efficiency and aimed to disrupt classroom time as little as possible. Consequently, there is rarely time for polite conversation and ancillary discussions, and usually the matter at hand is raised immediately. Because of these time constraints, educators tend to "dump" all of the information needed to be discussed at once. Typically, we go around the table and report out observations, test scores, and concerns with little to no discussion.

It is important that in our efforts to be thorough and efficient, we do not bury the parents in too much information too fast. It doesn't help them understand the big picture, and it often confuses even the small pieces of the issue that need to be addressed. Far too often parents are overwhelmed with the educational lingo and sheer volume of information we dump on them. The "deer in the headlights" look is usually a good sign that we've covered too much too quickly.

We recall a situation in which several staff members had gathered to discuss the program of Felicia, a 13-year-old student with a disability, who required the services of a special education teacher and several related service providers. Staff members were to summarize their assessments and recommendations for Felicia's program. It quickly became obvious that the amount and nature of the information was overwhelming the mother. After the third person finished her report, the mother's eyes were tearing up, and we knew we had to change our approach. The chairperson suddenly broke in, recapped what was said about Felicia's strengths, and asked the remaining staff, in the interest of "time and knowing that written reports would be made available," to simply list Felicia's strengths and explain the skills needing improvement. The relief in the mother's eyes was evident to all in the room.

Unless you've been in a parent's shoes, it may be difficult to understand the heightened sense of fear or anxiety that a parent feels when coming to a parent-teacher meeting, particularly one centered on problems and concerns the school may have. I am a professional speech therapist, a special educator with years of experience, and a knowledgeable diagnostician of learning problems. Yet none of this knowledge or experience prepared me for the first diagnostic meeting I attended for my grandson. On the way to the meeting, I had to pull my car over to stop shaking with fear. During the meeting, I had a constant feeling of nausea, and my ears were ringing. Even though I had pretty much diagnosed all of John Michael's problems, I was terrified that I missed something that would devastate me and my daughter. Fortunately, that wasn't the case, and we got through the meeting without a meltdown. I'm still not certain I heard every word said at that meeting!

That meeting taught me a lot about the need for the "no dump truck" rule. Taking time to stop and reflect and for parental input is necessary. Checking for understanding and periodically asking if there are any questions help to slow the delivery and allow for processing of the information shared. Observing parents carefully to determine if you have dumped too much at one time—and pulling back if you have—is crucial.

RULE 6: DOCUMENT

Document, document, document, and then document some more. The best way to solidify trust is to make sure that developments critical to the student's success happening in and out of the classroom are documented. While this does take time, carefully recorded documentation shared with all stakeholders ultimately saves time in the long run.

Documentation needs to be clear and specific. *Be the camera* and help parents *see* the situation as it happened. Make sure that what is recorded is observable, objective, factual, and not reflective of your interpretation. Leave subjective comments and judgments out of the record. Parents are more likely to have a clearer understanding of the behavior if it's documented objectively and clearly describes the situation (e.g., "John screamed 'Drop dead you pig!'"). Reporting the same incident subjectively (e.g., "John yelled inappropriately") is vague and open for interpretation. Objective recording of events, conversations, and information reduces the amount of interpretation that can be argued.

Spiral notebooks are wonderful for event documentation. They keep things in order of time and frequency and carefully document events in a manner that doesn't allow anyone to add information after the fact or forget information that might be critical to problem solving later on.

It is especially important to have complete documentation on students whose issues or families pose a challenge to the school-home relationship. If you are presented with negative or hostile communications, warned by previous teachers that a family is difficult, or if the issues surrounding the child are contentious (e.g., behavioral problems, possible disciplinary action, multiple academic failures, parents who demand high grades or specific homework delineations), you need to immediately set up a documentation system. All schoolwork, issues, contacts with parents, collaborative meetings on the students' behalf, and so on need to be carefully and objectively documented. Making *Be the camera* your mantra will help ensure that anyone reading your documentation will have the facts and not assumptions, feelings, or ideology. If all else fails, your documentation is evidence of actual events, remedial strategies tried, communications attempted, and all of your endeavors to help the child.

RULE 7: BE PREPARED

Before engaging in a discussion with parents, it is important to have all the relevant information about what is going to be discussed. Gather relevant information about a situation from each person who was involved. Obtain as much background information as possible before a commitment or decision is made based on less than thorough information.

Essentially, you need to make sure that you have done your homework. The best way to garner trust with parents is to show them your knowledge base. Prove that you have put time and effort into acquiring as much information as possible before approaching them with concerns, ideas, or thoughts about their child or home. In short, show them that you care enough to investigate all angles and come prepared with data and ideas.

Make it a practice to find out as much as you can about the child before the meeting. Call the previous teacher or school district and talk to teachers or the principal about the child. Ask about the level of parent involvement and what was learned about family needs and issues. Talking teacher to teacher is the best way to get valuable and pertinent information that may provide insight and solutions to a current problem.

Preparation ahead of time allows you to generate ideas and organize your thoughts and information. Being prepared helps you to arrange the meeting, be ready for any new related information and issues, and convey confidence in your discussion. All of this will help to facilitate the development of trust between you and parents.

RULE 8: "I DON'T KNOW"

When you don't know how to address an issue or respond to a question, don't be afraid to admit to a parent that you don't have all the answers. Simply say, "I don't know" or "I'm not sure." Be honest and willing to admit that you're stymied or need to get the answers and come back with more information or ideas.

Working through the problem-solving process with parents can be one of the best ways to develop a positive relationship. What you are doing is making them an active partner in your quest to do what is best for their child. Not only does it show respect, but it often leads to decisions and strategic plans that are far better than any you might have come up with on your own or solely with educators.

One parent was so taken aback when told "We don't know, what do *you* think?" that he not only searched for some workable solutions but became quite helpful from that point on. He commented that he had never been told by an educator that *he* might have some answers that would help *them.* It validated his worth to the process and the teachers and went a long way toward establishing a trusting relationship.

Another approach that we once used involved a middle school parent who wanted to know how we would handle his son if the student presented some of his most erratic behaviors in school. When he described what happens at home, we said, "We're not sure. How do you handle that type of behavior at home?" When he explained his method and its success, we complimented him and exchanged some ideas on how it could be used in a modified way at school. Together we also explored other ways that might be considered in the school setting. He thanked us for listening to his ideas and for allowing him to be part of the process of developing a behavioral plan for his son.

RULE 9: NEVER SAY *NEVER*

Nothing will crush a positive relationship with parents faster than telling them that their child will *never* do something. We don't want to take their dreams away. We don't have the right to trample on their hopes and aspirations for their child. We certainly don't have the right to assume that we are all-knowing.

In one group meeting with 15 administrators, we asked them for the single most prevalent cause of "problem parents." To our (and their own) surprise, they responded in almost total unison: "unrealistic expectations!" When probed further, they all agreed that if the parents would just realize that their child would not be reaching the goals they demanded, they would be happier with the schools and teachers.

However, we believe it is a parent's job to expect the most, best, and highest level of achievement possible for their child. We should expect nothing less. Our job is to clearly recognize those expectations and help parents understand where their child currently is and how far he or she will need to go to reach those expectations. It is our responsibility to delineate the intermediate steps that will need to be reached before their expectations can be realized.

Over the years, we have witnessed countless students reach levels and achievements they were "never" supposed to have reached. Students have passed courses that parents or teachers felt were out of reach for that child. One of the most inflammatory *nevers* cited by parents has to do with the probability of a child's academic future. "He will never go to college. He's not college material" is an all-too-common statement made by teachers, counselors, and administrators, particularly in the middle to high school levels. In fact, one of the authors was told this about her son, who now holds *two* advanced college degrees. The mother of another one of the authors was told that college was "not in the picture" for her daughter!

One student we worked with was a virtual nonreader in junior high. His parents had expressed hope that he might learn to read, but all attempts thus far had failed. His teacher wouldn't give up on his ability to develop a number of reading skills. She spent time talking with the young man and discovered that he really wanted to learn to cook. He was taken to observe several cooking classes and was asked to describe what he saw. An illustrative plan of how something is made was developed. Using this plan over the semester, he became familiar with all aspects of the cooking process. He was able to recall measurements and names of items needed in cooking. A great deal of time was spent on this visual approach, and once the visual aid was no longer needed, words were introduced. By the end of the year, he was able to read simple recipes. His parents became his strongest advocates, and most importantly, he realized he could read independently.

In most cases, students succeed because someone believed they could overcome barriers and achieve their goals and, more importantly, that someone *told* them they could. Most often, it was either parents or insightful teachers who never gave up and believed anything was possible.

This idea also applies to telling a parent that a teacher, school, or district will "never" do something they are requesting. It is all too common for school personnel to tell parents what the district will and will not do. We have heard statements such as "Our district will never pay for another staff person to help" or "Our district will never have parent conferences on weekends." Even if you believe it to be true, don't say it. Circumstances always have the potential to alter hard-and-fast rules, practices, and beliefs. By allowing for the possibility, you are, in effect, telling that parent that their child or family might be a special circumstance and need some modification of the norm. Whether or not anything changes, you've allowed for the possibility and demonstrated your interest in the individual needs of this student and family.

RULE 10: NEVER LIE

Dishonesty is the fastest way to dissolve a relationship and destroy any semblance of trust between parties. Direct untruths, fibs, and exaggerations are all forms of dishonesty. Omissions of critical information that lead others to inappropriate conclusions or ideas are also lies that can be very destructive to the relationship.

Owning up to your mistakes or inappropriate actions can garner trust with parents. Being truthful and openly admitting mistakes makes us more "human." It allows for future interactions to be more honest, without the burden of the lie getting in the way of candid and open communication between school and home.

It's no secret that teachers, administrators, and schools won't have all the answers or be able to prevent problems from arising. Nor should it be a surprise to parents that school personnel can make mistakes in solving problems that do arise. What *does* surprise them, however, is when teachers or administrators openly admit that a mistake was made and then give some assurances that similar mistakes will not be made in the future.

Some of the best parent-school relationships are forged after a mistake has been admitted. Trust is strengthened once lines of communication are shared openly and productively and a process is put in place to significantly reduce the opportunity for a similar mistake to be made again.

In one particularly difficult and unusual situation, a ninth-grade student was disciplined for throwing the "*F*-bomb" at his math teacher. Per school discipline policy, the offense was punishable with a three-day suspension. The principal made the call to the parents explaining the situation and consequences. Later in the day, the principal received additional information from other students that indicated the suspended young man was provoked by the teacher. Upon thorough investigation and admittance by the teacher that he had, indeed, made an error in judgment by calling the student a "dirt bag" just prior to the student's remark, it was decided that both teacher and student were in the wrong, would apologize to each other, and the suspension would be lifted. The teacher called the parents, explained honestly what had happened, apologized, and stated it would never happen again. The suspension was rescinded. The next day, the parents phoned the principal and, while not happy with the incident, said they respected the teacher's honesty and were confident it wouldn't happen again.

Another example that comes to mind involved the use of a middle school library by special education students in self-contained classrooms. A group of parents were outraged that their children "could not have a library period" like all other classrooms in the building. The law called for equal access, and their children were being denied that right. Upon investigation, it was discovered that the building had made a mistake in not securing picture books and lower-level readers to accommodate the significantly lower reading levels of the classes, and the librarian simply didn't have anything to show them or work with them on. Mea culpas were given to the parents, books were immediately ordered, and the librarian was loaned some appropriate books so that the special education classrooms could be scheduled into library classes immediately.

Because the principal admitted her oversight and worked swiftly to correct the problem, this negative situation gave rise to an active parent group that became an ongoing collaborative effort between parents and the district. This collaboration went a long way toward garnering trust in the administration and the positive intent of the school district. This group went on to identify and solve many school and home issues with both groups providing support and resources to each other. Issues such as transportation, testing, communication, placement, and community resources were explored and resolved to the benefit of the children. Communications remained honest and open, trust was established, and the "never lie" rule was openly expressed and valued by both sides.

SUMMARY

Respect and trust are crucial to the development of positive relationships. Making sure that there are common practices and courtesies that parents and teachers can rely on is fundamental. Following the specific rules discussed in this chapter will serve to facilitate the formation of a basic foundation of trust between home and school.

When these basic principles are adhered to, parents and teachers respond positively and a better working relationship can evolve. To the contrary, violating any of these rules can serve to break trust or confidence between home and school.

Using Flexibility to Enhance Relationships

Innovation distinguishes between a leader and a follower.

—Steve Jobs

Life is increasingly complicated for many families, requiring flexibility in educators' thinking, actions, and beliefs. Compromises must be made when forming any relationship, and parents and families are no exception. Some compromises are relatively easy to make, while others may cost time and effort.

As previously discussed, strong parent-school relationships are critical to students' academic success. Therefore, we *must* find ways to deviate from our norm when the norm fails, and we have to exert more effort and creativity to forge some relationships.

Teachers cannot and should not bear the sole responsibility of finding creative solutions to forming and maintaining positive relationships with parents in the face of significant family issues. The strategies and techniques discussed below are meant as considerations for teachers, building administrators, and district office personnel for increasing parental involvement. Administrators need to be supportive and helpful in allotting teachers the time and flexibility to deal with these issues.

COMMON FAMILY ISSUES NEEDING ACCOMMODATION

Time Constraints

In many families, both parents are working or one parent is working multiple jobs. As a result, the amount of time that a parent can give to attend school meetings may be severely limited or nonexistent. In recognition of this, many schools have extended their typical afternoon and evening conference times to include early-morning and late-night hours. However, for many families, these time extensions are still not compatible with their work schedules.

Time constraints make it difficult to meet with or even phone parents. Yet it is critical that you make the time to meet with parents whenever and wherever possible. Holding parent meetings on weekends (with flex time given back to teachers willing to do so), conducting phone conferences whenever the parent is available, and giving release time to teachers during the day for parent meetings are all methods we found effective for addressing time constraints.

In one instance, we were able to work out an agreement with a local employer of several of our parents. With the employer's permission, we held mini parent conferences at the parents' job site during their break or lunchtime. The employer allowed us to set up a "conference afternoon" in the staff workroom and set schedules so that the parents could use their breaks to meet with us. The parents were grateful that we would go to such lengths to accommodate them, and the employer was impressed that the school district cared enough to send its teachers to the work site and was considerate enough to keep to the allotted meeting time limits. It was a win-win since the employer didn't need to accommodate staff time off and parents were allowed to be a part of their child's education without losing money by missing work.

Time constraints also interfere with parents' ability to assist with homework, get students off to school, or make sure they get to bed at a reasonable time. Older siblings are often responsible for the parenting duties early in the morning or at bedtime. If you can assist with homework or scheduling accommodations that will not punish the older sibling, that will go a long way toward forging a positive relationship with the family.

One specific older sibling situation comes to mind. We had a young man in ninth grade that was always late for school. He consistently missed part or all of his first-period English class. Once his tardiness reached the disciplinary level of the principal's office, the situation was exposed. His mother had to report to work at 6:30 a.m. at a local hospital. His younger sister had to board her elementary school bus at 7:50. Once this ninth grader got her on the bus and ran to school, he was 15 minutes late—or missed the first class entirely. There was nothing the family could do. We had a divorced mother, two kids, no money for a babysitter, and no neighbors willing or able to help on a daily basis. A simple trip to the guidance office, a small switch in his schedule from English to study hall, and an understanding that we would tolerate his being late for study hall as long as his home situation remained the same was the answer. The result was that this young man's overall attendance improved, he was more attentive in all his classes, and his grades improved.

Other ideas for getting around time constraints include the following:

- Setting up a notebook system for parent-school correspondence that regularly travels between home and school
- Providing parents with a schedule of when you are available to talk if they need or want to call
- Providing parents with school (not personal) e-mail addresses for corresponding with teachers and administrators
- Consider sending out e-mail blasts notifying all parents of upcoming events, special awards, or important reminders

Financial Problems

While our public school system provides "free" education for all children, some states and school districts depend on family contributions to help pay for items such as supplemental school supplies and field trips. These requirements get in the way of relationships between school and home. Put simply, 18.2 percent of children under the age of 18 in the United States are living in families with earnings at or below the conservative poverty line (U.S. Census Bureau, 2007). Not only are these families often unable to make a financial contribution to their children's education, the lack of quality health care and nutrition can and does get in the way of optimal learning. For example, many children who need glasses don't have them. Our families that are struggling financially, have inadequate living conditions, or lack health care are at a disadvantage in our school system. Typically, we can provide free and reduced-cost lunch and breakfast programs and PTO-supported field trips. School nurses (if available) can at least provide assistance in determining if a child needs to be sent home or seen by a doctor.

Some of our families may require us to go above and beyond our typical efforts. We may need to find ways to provide students with books or supplies for school and home use. We might want to approach our local community groups to get glasses for students who need them but can't afford them. We may want to ask them to sponsor students financially so that the children can participate in school events. While schools can't do it all, at the very least we should explore and compile a directory of local resources that can provide the financial support necessary for our students' success.

One teacher I know spent her own time helping parents apply for Medicaid and state health services for their families. Her daughter worked for the state system and the daughter's intimate knowledge of it was of great benefit to many families in her school. The parents were very grateful, and as a result, the students were healthier and missed less school, were more attentive when there, and a stronger bond was formed between school and home.

Another teacher took advantage of school breaks to have her students (and any others who wanted to) clean out their lockers before heading home. She stood by the front door with large garbage cans, and the students dropped their unwanted stuff into them before leaving. She then went through them and culled the still-usable paper, pens, pencils, and notebooks and gave the recycled items to those who needed supplies. It was amazing how many nice things were discarded and how grateful the needy students were to receive them.

It is important that we remain conscious of and sensitive to the economic impositions we place on struggling families. Other ways to financially assist with our educational endeavors include the following:

- School sales for specific events (e.g., bake sales, craft sales, garage sales)
- Student fundraising events such as car washes and recycling collections
- Tapping into local service clubs such as Rotary, Masons, and YMCA to support educational efforts
- Asking local businesses to partner with the school by sponsoring or helping to fund school events

Divorce or Separation

Divorces or separations range from amicable to extremely hostile. In all cases, it is imperative that the school fully understands the specific legal situation of each divorced couple (i.e., custody, visitation, parental rights). We know that court mandates *must* be honored despite what we may think of a judgment or of what a parent might want. The school and teacher must respect legal judgments and adhere to court orders.

Legal mandates should be clearly articulated and their adherence by the school should be nonnegotiable. This may make maintaining a positive relationship with both parents, at times, very difficult. However, both parents must understand that the school is not taking sides and is just making sure it follows court judgments.

Keeping the child's interests front and center will go a long way toward garnering a favorable school-parent relationship. In contentious divorce situations, it is critical to make sure you keep the child off the battlefield and fight all urges to take sides with one parent or the other. Parents may be "shooting at" each other, but the child should not be the unintended target. With the support of the administration or social workers, this concern should be clearly articulated with both parents. Time should be taken to discuss how their relationship may be affecting their child's educational well-being. Almost always, both parents have the best interests of their child in mind, and sometimes, a simple reminder of that is all that is needed.

Sometimes, a situation will present itself in which your only option may be confrontation. Constructive confrontation is intended to increase the self-awareness of the person(s) being confronted. Three ways to do so are describing the parent's behavior and its impact, pointing out inconsistencies in what is said and what is done, and identifying discrepancies between intent and action. The confrontation is not intended to change the other person but to create the circumstance(s) in which it is possible to change.

In one particularly nasty divorce situation during my tenure as a principal, I had to physically intervene between two parents who were face-to-face screaming at each other at a school event. I literally brought both parents into my office and reflected to both what I (and others, including their son) had witnessed, heard, and felt at their display of hostility. I further added how their open animosity might be negatively impacting their six-year-old son's ability to perform academically and socially. I appealed to their common love of their child to stop fighting in front of him—at home or school. Their son reported to me weeks later that "Mommy and Daddy are being nicer to each other," and his behavior and academic success improved.

Although it takes more time and requires more flexibility, it is a good idea to meet with divorced parents separately. While it might be double duty, it will yield better results. You will often get a better picture of what the child is dealing with from both sides that may be impacting his or her ability to function and learn in the classroom. Also, separated and divorced parents tend to be more open and honest in their communications without the other there to "critique" their statements.

It is important that your communications with both parents (if the court allows it) are nondiscriminatory. To foster parental involvement, we suggest that all school communiqués (e.g., newsletters, report cards, event notices) be given to both parents. They can be mailed to the non-custodial parent if necessary. Making sure that both parents are well informed increases the chances of a positive relationship with both, and the parental support of school efforts on behalf of the child is doubled.

Emotional Support

Many of our families are coping with emotionally draining situations, resulting in roadblocks between home and school. Some of the most common situations involve failing students, students with disabilities, families who are in the process of separation or divorce, families who are dealing with the illness or death of a close family member, non-English-speaking families, families who struggle with reading, or single parents trying to do the work of two.

FAILING STUDENTS

All parents want their children to succeed. When parents receive notification that their child is in danger of failing or has failed, they often will experience a sense of loss accompanied by denial, guilt, or anger with the situation. They might blame the school or their child for the problem, or they might struggle with their own sense of failure.

It is important to understand that these parents may need our emotional support as we work through the underlying causes of the failure. We need objective information that will bring us to a shared understanding of the problem and allow us to collaborate on possible remedies. Problem solving is critical to this support. We cannot leave the family with failure as the end product. Through cooperative development of a plan, you will provide the parent with positive support and a sense of hope that the situation is temporary and can be resolved.

STUDENTS WITH DISABILITIES

Having worked with families of students with disabilities (and my having been the mother and grandmother of two such students), we can absolutely attest to the fact that school can be a frightening and anxiety-producing encounter for both children and parents. The educational model and process for dealing with students with disabilities is based on a deficiency model. It focuses on a child's weaknesses and needs. It requires us to delineate the remediation plan for each area of weakness and articulate how far the child needs to go. This deficiency model forces us to lead with the negative, and time constraints often do not let us explore all of the really positive aspects of the child. We inadvertently leave the parent feeling defeated.

Change the mind-set. Break the pattern. Lead with the positive, always. It is critical to exemplify the successes, positive situations, and encouraging events surrounding the child. Focus on these strengths, accentuate the positives, and compliment honestly where compliments are due. By leading with the child's strengths, both you and the parents can focus on the value of their child's emotional, physical, and educational strengths. Following that, you can then provide strong emotional support for discussions on the impact of their child's disability and its educational, social, and emotional consequences.

FAMILIES OF DIVORCE OR SEPARATION

Parents going through a divorce need to feel good as parents. Make sure that you highlight the positive things you see in their child and attribute them to their parenting where you see the fit. If and when you learn of a particular hardship the custodial parent might be facing (e.g., finances, health care, living arrangements), try to locate community resources that might be able to provide support. Anything you can do to let these parents know that you understand what is happening and are willing to help will be a valuable tool in forging a more positive relationship.

Custodial arrangements can have an adverse impact on children's physical and emotional well-being and, as a result, their ability to perform in school. The school may need to adjust its homework policy to accommodate a child's living situation (e.g., no homework when the child is with the parent who cannot or will not provide assistance). The school may need to monitor the child's physical and emotional health, behavior, performance in school, or attendance following each living situation. The goal is to keep the child's interests at the forefront and talk with each parent about what is observed and how it is impacting their child's learning.

Our children of separation or divorce are often at the mercy of the courts and whatever arrangements the judges have made. In one particular case, Simon, a six-year-old boy, was placed under a joint-custody agreement that was having an extremely negative impact on his emotional, physical, and educational well-being. The judge had determined that because both parents lived in the same neighborhood, Simon would switch parents every other day. Needless to say, Simon never knew where he was going, became confused and angry, and started to demonstrate aggressive behavior in school. Neither parent liked the arrangement, but they felt there was nothing they could do. We brought both parents in; composed a letter from the school administration, teacher, school nurse, and both parents; and asked for a modification to the order based on the effects it was having on Simon. The judge agreed, and a more typical arrangement was arrived at, giving Simon consistency throughout the school week and equal time with each parent.

ILLNESS OR DEATH OF A CLOSE FAMILY MEMBER

The illness or death of a close family member or friend can be a devastating event for a family. It takes time for the family to move through the grieving process, and at times, the event itself takes over the ability for any or all of the family members to function well. Providing emotional support for a family in crisis is crucial.

The school does not need to know intimate details of a friend's or family member's death or illness. It simply needs to know the dynamic is occurring and provide support to the child and, if possible, family as necessary (e.g., counseling, time-outs to deal with emotions that rise to the surface). This support can come in many forms. You can provide an ear to listen to the grieving person, the time to attend a wake or funeral, or the kindness of sending a note or card expressing your concern and support. Simply letting families know that you understand their pain and are willing to work around the results of the situation (e.g., absences or tardiness, increased behavioral issues) will let the family know that you empathize and care about them.

NON-ENGLISH-SPEAKING
AND LOW-LITERACY FAMILIES

As our schools become more culturally diverse, we are encountering increased numbers of non-English-speaking families or families in which the adult members are unable to read English. This poses a significant strain on the family and presents a real challenge for the schools when these families are asked and expected to support school efforts. Our communiqués often go unread or misunderstood by our parents, causing confusion and making partnerships nearly impossible.

Schools need to make sure that parents can understand what is being communicated to them. We cannot assume that the children will adequately translate the information (especially when the information is negative!). It is important that schools try their best to directly communicate with all parents as best they can.

Obviously, it may be impossible for communiqués to be sent out in every language a school might have to accommodate. However, if a school is faced with a considerable population of a specific nationality, it is incumbent upon it to find a way to accommodate the language of that nationality *if they want to forge positive relationships with that group of parents.*

I worked with one school district that was approaching a 35 percent Hispanic population. The parent group was, as a whole, angry with the district and dismayed with the lack of communication they were given. Upon talking with them and analyzing the specifics of their concerns, it became apparent that they were particularly upset with the secondary level over disciplinary actions. The school would call home and tell them that their child was suspended or had gotten into a fight, and then, when explaining the situation in English, the specifics were lost. The parents felt powerless to assist their child or understand what had happened.

It was suggested to the district that it locate from within or hire from outside at least one person in each building (e.g., secretary, aide, custodian) who was fluent in Spanish and could act as an interpreter when needed. The district immediately canvassed its staffs and, where necessary, hired an additional staff person who could function as an interpreter whenever necessary. These staff also translated brochures and newsletters into Spanish. By making a concerted effort to address this primary issue, all of this was done within a month of the parent meeting. Relationships immediately improved, parent involvement in school increased, and several parents went on to become primary advocates of the district.

COUNTERPRODUCTIVE FAMILY DYNAMICS

Schools are a microcosm of society. We all carry around emotional baggage. Students are no different. We know that some of our families are in significant crises. These crises are causing family dynamics to be counterproductive to their child's educational needs. Among the most common issues are physical and sexual abuse, alcoholism and drug abuse, legal problems that can be criminal, and financial situations that cause evictions and a high rate of mobility.

Rules and regulations, processes, and school procedures are often disregarded by families whose daily lives have caused them to become dysfunctional or counterproductive. Yet it is exactly the children of these situations who need our help most. We must find a way to deal with the family, provide as much support as feasible, and minimize the negative effects of this dysfunction on the child's educational program.

School demands can add significant stressors to an already stressed family. We expect that students will do their homework, get the support and assistance they need at home, come to school on time, and behave appropriately despite whatever emotional issues may be affecting them at home. Yet it is precisely these issues of homework, behavior, attention, and attendance that can provide us with the indicators of problematic family dynamics.

As chairpersons of the building-level student-intervention teams, we quickly observed a pattern developing as student after student was brought to the team by teachers struggling with these students in their classes. A high percentage of these students were failing to do their homework, missing school frequently, or not paying attention in class. Upon discussion of home and family, time and time again highly emotional family situations arose. Financial problems; alcoholism; legal problems; physical, sexual, or drug abuse; or other significant disrupters of safe home environments were uncovered.

SUMMARY

While it is not in our domain to pry into significant family matters, it *is* our responsibility to try to understand the factors that might be impacting a student's ability to learn. When we discover family dynamics that are counterproductive to the learning environment (e.g., time, money, health, divorce, cultural, legal issues), it behooves us to use our creativity and, when needed, seek alternative ways to help and support students in their learning environment. We might need to compromise and show flexibility with students who are experiencing these types of interfering issues in their home lives. We might need to use other sources of support (e.g., social worker, school nurse, child protective services) to assist our efforts to help the child and perhaps extend that help to the family as a whole. The bottom line is that we need to think about what factors might be impinging on our students' school performance. We can't expect our students to leave their problems at home and not manifest them in some way at school. To ignore this and not flex where possible is, in our opinion, educational malpractice.

Documenting
and Celebrating
School Events

The memories your customers have of your company will determine its future success or failure.

—David Freemantle

When I read newspaper articles and listen to discussions about education, it frustrates and disappoints me that almost all of the talk is focused on the negative issues and problems we are faced with in our schools. News coverage rarely celebrates all of the wonderful things going on daily in classrooms all over the country. As a teacher and then administrator, I was often amazed at how most of the parental contacts I had were negative—often complaints about something the school shouldn't have done or something the school failed to do that it should have.

As we reflect on the general impressions of our educational system, it occurs to us that at least some of this negative focus is our own fault. We have failed to document and celebrate the numerous positive things that are happening every day in every school across the country. We do make general attempts to showcase our special events and awards and honors, but we fail to show parents (and our communities) the literally hundreds of things we do that lead to constructive results and huge successes in the lives of the children under our care.

It is imperative that we take the time and put forth the effort to showcase our educational practices and demonstrate to our families that we are working hard and making a positive difference in the lives of their children. If we want to build bridges and forge positive relationships with parents, then we must demonstrate to them that our hard work and efforts are making things happen on a daily basis that will benefit their children. We need to build confidence and trust in what we are doing. We need to increase our parents' knowledge of educational issues and practices, encourage more parental involvement in our activities, and solicit more support for our practices.

Educators are not trained to market themselves. They are not in the business of "tooting their own horns." But we need to be. We need to show families that we are doing our very best, and with their help, the outcomes will be positive and perhaps even spectacular. We need to demonstrate that by working as a team, home and school can bring about the academic, social, and behavioral progress that all of us desire and expect from our educational system.

So, where do we begin with our documentation plan? What is it that we are supposed to document? When should we document it? Where should we put this documentation? Once we document, should we celebrate? If so, what, why, how, when, and where should we celebrate?

We all know that documenting academic progress is necessary. Grading and testing are the two areas that dominate our thoughts, fill the news, and form the basis of a school's evaluation. That is not what we are talking about in this chapter. Here, we are talking about documenting and celebrating all of the learning activities that lead students to be better academically, socially, and behaviorally in and out of school. Since most children, when asked by their parents what they did in school that day, say *nothing*, it is left to us to alter that notion.

WHAT DO WE NEED TO DOCUMENT?

One of the most frequent comments we hear from school visitors is a variation of "I had no idea teaching involved so much, that it demanded so much attention to so many things." Everyone knows that teachers teach and then test what was taught. We expect that homework, quizzes, and tests will tell the tale of what did or didn't happen in the classroom. But people have no idea that, in addition to academics, teachers are constantly striving to improve social, behavioral, personal, and learning issues that interfere with the content being taught.

Think about the time and energy spent on creating workable student groups, the process of thinking through what is heard or seen, the interpersonal relationships that form (or aren't forming) within the class, or the constant need to attend to behaviors that interrupt or facilitate the learning process. It has been said that the average teacher makes about eight thousand (yes, eight *thousand*) decisions a day. It's no small wonder that we're tired at the end of the day! In addition, there's the time and energy needed to create large activities like plays, presentations, exhibits, and open houses.

Simply put, we need to record almost everything we do in our efforts to help the children under our charge grow. The more evidence we can provide of what we actually do on a daily basis, the stronger the bond will become between home and school. Documenting a student's work, efforts, behavior, attitude, attention, and progress will help parents understand the wide range of teacher attention and assistance provided toward realizing a child's potential.

Time (or lack thereof) is our nemesis. We are often so busy with everything we must do that we can't (or don't) document or celebrate our efforts, or even the child's progress, as much as we should. We'd like to share with you some of the more creative, uncomplicated, and successful practices we've employed, or seen employed, that garnered positive parental feedback.

QUICK, EASY, AND ROUTINE DAILY DOCUMENTATION METHODS

The fundamental elements of good documentation are detailed content, time specific (i.e., dated), tied to targets or standards communicated to parents, and dependability (i.e., can be counted on to appear). Parents' confidence will increase as they understand clearly what the classroom priorities are. Be sure to clarify the standards and explain what is expected from their child. Once this is done, your documentation will then explain where their child is, how he or she is progressing, and what you are working on, looking for, and monitoring.

All teachers look for and need to find quick and easy ways to document what's happening in the classroom. These will need to be recorded and used for later discussion, reports, assessments, and evaluation of classroom work. Finding processes that can be systematized and provide clear, descriptive records with less time and effort is crucial to a successful documentation system. Below you will find a few such processes.

Quick Notes

For this method, you will be leaving 3×5 index cards in specific locations around the classroom. Use color-coded cards for different kinds of notes, for example, red for behavior notes, green for math notes, and white for reading. The idea is to make notes as you teach or move around the room on whatever needs attention—how a student is doing, problems—while in that area. These are not meant to be narrative. Use lists to quickly note things like, "10/15: Patty G. read well" or "Sam V. couldn't sound out 3 syllables." You could have one card per student or group.

Another quick-note process is to have 3×5 index cards taped on students' desks with specific items to be quickly checked by the teacher as he or she notes their behavior regarding cooperation, attention to task, following directions, participating, and volunteering answers. You could have individualized items that target specific goals for each child. Date the cards (some teachers do daily cards and some weekly) and keep the originals for your records. Then send copies home for parents to monitor progress in the target areas.

Communication Notebook on Desk

Communication notebooks are a wonderful tool for all teachers to use to communicate back and forth with home. Special education teachers use communication notebooks en masse because, for many students with special communication needs, the only information the parents get about school is that which comes directly from the teacher. General education teachers are discovering that this type of communication assists with accuracy, problem solving, and timeliness of response to issues and requests. Yet teachers rightfully fear the time it will take to write out narrative communications for every child and sometimes don't (or won't) employ them as much as they could.

Spiral communication notebooks are very useful in establishing a handy and efficient way to maintain back-and-forth communications between home and school. Not only will you be able to keep detailed documentation on myriad issues as they arise, you will be able to note progress checkpoints that the child reaches. The key to using the spiral notebook is to keep it chronological. That way, you have a long-range view of how the year has gone and how the child is progressing in the various areas you have targeted.

One of the best uses of the spiral notebook we've seen is with teachers who use one per student. The notebook is kept on the top corner of the student's desk, and there is an expectation that the teacher will occasionally stop, note something quickly, and move on. The student then brings the notebook home for the parents to read and initial.

The key to this is for teachers to make a quick note (no long narratives) of things they wanted to share or celebrate with parents (e.g., "Valerie got a 92 on her spelling test today!") or things the child needs to do (e.g., "Bobby needs to bring a raincoat tomorrow for our field trip"). Notes to parents to set up a phone conference or as a reminder of an upcoming meeting can also be communicated.

One teacher used this idea in a slightly different manner. She employed a large, spiral notebook that she alphabetically tabbed by student name. She would find the child's section, quickly date and note whatever she was looking to note, and move on. This notebook was then copied and used at parent meetings or conferences to show progress noted as time went on. A variation of this theme is to have tabbed, color-coded spiral notebooks for each subject area and one for behavior and participation.

Sticky Notes

An entire book could be written about how, when, and where teachers use sticky notes in the classroom to enhance their instructional practices. Here, we focus on using them to document and celebrate student success in the classroom. They are easy to carry around; fun to stick on students, their communication books, or planners; and because of the bright colors they come in, are easy to spot and remember to use.

It helps that sticky notes are small. It forces us to be succinct in our message. Simple phrases like "Great job: 100 on spelling test" or "Wonderful teamwork" not only recognize the student's efforts and success but go a long way toward improving student self-esteem. Success breeds success, and acknowledging and celebrating a child's success can only lead to more positive outcomes. Imagine how a parent will react when their child arrives home "sticky noted"!

I remember one unforgettable example of this. I was principal of an elementary school, and Jason, age 10, was sent down to the office to see me at the end of the day. The teacher phoned and told me he was on his way. Since this student was a "frequent flyer" of my office, I expected the worst. I heard my secretary laughing, and when I looked up, there he was, covered in sticky notes. He asked me to read them. As I did, I realized that this child had had one wonderful, terrific, all-together positive day. He had "paid attention in science," "volunteered information," "helped Meghan with her artwork," "finished his math work," "answered questions in music class," and "listened carefully in oral reading." I got my camera, took several pictures of him, and later put them on my wall. I didn't see him in my office for quite some time after that as he continued to try his best to "get his stickers."

Point Charts

Teachers are getting very proficient at using point charts to articulate a student's progress in just about any academic arena. These charts are quick and easy checkmark systems to note when a child has successfully achieved or demonstrated a target goal(s). There are homework charts, good-listener charts, completed-work charts, cooperation charts, and whatever else you come up with. Some charts will have several target qualities across the y-axis, with student names listed on the x-axis so that comparisons can be made. Some teachers make individual charts or "contract charts" displaying specific target goals that the child needs to show improvement on. The next step is to make sure that those charts are shared with parents.

Point charts are valuable because they create a routine, and expectations are clear and consistent over time. They are great conversation starters with parents. We suggest that you put up your point chart system (or actual charts) at the start-of-school open house. Take the time to explain to parents why the targets are important. Put in simple terms how meeting those targets will improve their child's classroom success. Finally, suggest ways that they might help to support those targets at home. You might even want to suggest that a corresponding chart be put up at home!

The best example of a point system process that we came across was in a fourth-grade inclusive classroom with a heterogeneous group of students. The teacher made sure that she carefully explained the point charts by discussing why each target behavior or goal was critical to the success of her students. Each parent took a copy of an empty chart home with them to keep as a reminder of the goals the class was working on. She told the parents that their child's completed chart would come home at the end of each month. She then had a discussion with the parents about how they might help support the goals at home. Together, they came up with ideas and suggestions and discussed their thoughts on the goals themselves. The empty chart and ideas and suggestions from the open-house discussion were then copied and sent home (with a simple letter of explanation) to all parents so that those who could not attend had the information.

WEEKLY OR MONTHLY NEWSLETTERS

Classrooms all over the country offer newsletters that go home to parents and are placed on the school Web site. Some are weekly and some monthly. In order to enhance the likelihood that they will be read, an effective strategy is to have the students write many of the articles. Not only does it spike the interest of parents, it's a great way to work on literacy skills and encourage students to write, draw, and talk about their experiences and ideas. Students with written-expression weaknesses can be given the opportunity to draw on their strengths (e.g., provide ideas and suggestions for articles, offer drawings, or bring in pictures to be used) and participate in the newsletter's production. The outcome is that parents see what is happening in the classroom, and all students get to showcase their skills and contributions through the newsletter.

One exemplary case of how newsletters can be a bridge between home and school occurred in our junior high school. We had an eighth-grade student with significant behavioral problems whose suspension rate was rising as the months progressed. I had frequent opportunity to talk with his parents, who consistently expressed their frustration with his inability to "do anything well." One day I noticed he was drawing in the in-school suspension room. The drawing was exquisitely detailed, with a beautiful rendition of a lake, an explosive sunset, and a wistful-looking woman staring at the water. I asked him where he learned to draw, and he just shrugged and said he taught himself.

I asked him if I could borrow the picture and then approached the teacher of our TAG (Talented and Gifted) program about her monthly newsletter. I showed her the picture and asked if there was any way that this young man could be part of the program as a sort of "artist in residence." She agreed, he was willing, and the association began. His artwork graced the cover of each newsletter from that point on, his behavior improved (because his participation in TAG was conditional on his behavior), and his teachers started to report improvement in attendance, participation, behavior, and effort. His parents called me to thank me for finding an avenue that excited and challenged their son. Most important, their cooperation with me and their contact with his teachers increased significantly.

SPECIALIZED DAILY CONTACTS

Daily contacts usually have a greater percentage of parental response than monthly, seasonal, or quarterly contacts. They tend to be more individualized and personal and therefore more likely to stimulate a response.

Technology has provided us with a quick avenue for contact with some parents. More and more parents, particularly our working professional parents, are asking that we contact them through e-mail because of heavy work schedules. However, while e-mails are becoming more common, caution needs to be taken with their use. We may find them quick and easy to send off, but they can easily become too numerous to respond to, parents' expectations on certainty or timeliness of responses can be overreached, and their tone and intent can be easily misinterpreted. We suggest limiting the number of e-mails you send or respond to and being careful with sending a response quickly. Make sure you have the time to think through what you are saying and review it carefully for tone, clarity, and message before hitting *send*.

Direct, positive phone calls work well to build bridges between home and school. One teacher we know tries to call five homes a day to note something positive that each of these five children has done recently. By doing so, the entire class can be covered in a week or so, and parents get to hear the good news coming from the classroom. Be sure to use the child's name and be specific with comments so that parents can be sure that you are really talking about their child (it's amazing how parents think we called the wrong house with *good* news), and they can reinforce that specific behavior at home. Don't be afraid to leave this kind of message on an answering machine if no one is at home. Parents have told me that they save these messages a while because they are so proud—and rarely will a child erase them!

Notes sent home on a daily basis can be generalized ahead of time and customized for the student on the day you wish to contact the parent with specifics. For example, you can create a set of note cards, or keep a file of note cards on your computer, that document specific behaviors and target goals that you want to record and send home quickly to parents. One such example was a teacher-made note that read as follows:

Dear _____ ,

I wanted you to know that _____ behavior was fantastic today. He listened, participated well in class, and did a great job with _____ .

Signed: _____

Date: _____

CONFERENCES

We all know that teacher conferences have significant time constraints, and there is only so much that we can do in a short period of time. Too often, we are forced to discuss problems that need to be addressed quickly, and we don't have enough time to showcase our work and that of the students. Yet we need to do just that if we are to build a strong bond and obtain a support network from home.

We strongly recommend that you keep work samples and create a portfolio for each student. Bring the portfolio with you to share with parents each time you meet with them. Many teachers use weekly folders or graded-paper folders to keep work samples in. Not only does a folder showcase the work, it reflects your attitudes and the priorities of your class and the student at hand. It demonstrates that, on an ongoing basis, you take the time to evaluate, collect, and organize the student's work.

Of equal importance is that you have a portfolio of sample work that meets the standards of the grade level. Explain the qualities of the standard and what skills are being developed. One note of caution: don't put the "best of the best" out there for parents of struggling students to compare with their child's work. Find samples that are good examples of the work for that grade level and discuss what you are hoping their child will be able to achieve. Talk about the kinds of activities you are engaged in to assist their child's progress toward the standards and, finally, discuss possible ways they can help at home.

Parents often stopped in to my office on their way out of the building after meeting with teachers. What I noted most was that those who left in a positive mood, regardless of the skill level of their child, were the parents who left feeling that the teacher was trying a lot of things, noting every bit of progress that their child had made, and focused on their child's strengths while working hard to attenuate their weaknesses. Showcasing your efforts and their positive effects on their child's progress will go a long way toward forging a stronger home connection.

DVDs/CDs

Visuals are a principal way to document and celebrate events that are happening in the classroom and school. Technology has made it not only easy but inexpensive to create visual memories and evidence of student achievement and success. Most families have DVD players, many have home computers, and the public library will allow families to play a DVD or CD for free. Schools that have parent libraries or parent conference rooms can make sure that a DVD or CD player is available at all times.

DVDs have been produced by schools to document school plays and major events. Holiday concerts, PTO fundraisers, sports, and academic competitions are just a few examples of what schools record on a regular basis. One school in our local area creates a DVD "memory" for each grade level that showcases the major happenings of the class throughout the year. Each student gets to take a copy home at the end of the school year.

It is equally, perhaps more, important for the teacher to visually document the multitude of activities that are created and presented throughout the year to help students grow. Explanations of the activity's purpose, its connection to the curriculum, and goals for the student(s) should be explained as part of the documentation. The end product becomes a record of the focus, effort, and priorities of the school year, as well as the success of the child.

One teacher we know makes an audiotape of each student as he or she reads aloud and answers questions about what the student has read. This is done at the beginning of the year, the middle, and the end of the year. The growth of the child is clearly evident. The parent can observe the amount of improvement, and a discussion about the degree and type of improvement made, as well as what is still needed, can lead to a better understanding of the reading process and the student's future direction.

BACK-TO-SCHOOL NIGHTS AND OPEN HOUSES

Traditional back-to-school nights or open houses typically involve teachers waiting in their rooms to discuss with parents what the year will be like, what the curriculum covers, and what expectations they have of their students. It's a meet-and-greet activity that, while providing information the parent needs, does little to showcase school events or the community of students that has formed for the new year.

A second kind of open house is built around student work, interests, and skills. One school we know themed their open houses each year. One year, they did an arts and sciences theme. Each classroom did short presentations with students showcasing posters, reports, laboratory experiments, and other creations. The art classes featured students doing different types of projects, while the music rooms and lobbies of the building held students playing instruments. Another year featured a "Technology Today" themed event. Students manned computers and video players in their rooms to demonstrate e-mail, Web surfing, and software used in learning, while students in the gym, art room, and music room used equipment to demonstrate techniques using digital readouts and settings to record progress.

One local school holds an open house four times a year in its gymnasium foyer. Unlike most gymnasium foyers that host the sports achievement awards of the school, this school expanded their focus. The foyer is set up like a museum lobby, and parents are invited to come in anytime to look at the art work and student writing samples framed on the walls and set on floor pedestals. Another school I visited sported professionally framed artwork done by its students over the years.

In our district, we started a tradition of having the district office showcase work samples from each of our school buildings. Each building took a month of the year and set up an exhibit of student work samples completed in any subject they chose. What started out as artwork samples rapidly grew to samples of math, language arts, science, and social studies. Parents and community members often dropped by the district office just to see what changed at the beginning of the month. It was common to hear comments about the amazing things kids were studying and doing at each of the grade levels. Positive feelings led to increased community participation in budget votes and stronger ties between school and home.

SUMMARY

We need to make sure parents are given a multitude of communications and myriad opportunities to know and understand the types of learning activities that their children are engaged in while under our care. We cannot and should not be talking to parents only or mostly when problems arise with their child. Therefore, it is critical that we develop and use many ways to document and display the progress their child makes academically, socially, behaviorally, and interpersonally.

A number of children will show consistent growth and great success in all areas. Others will be generally successful with perhaps only one or two areas with which they had struggled. Another group will have challenges in one or more areas that need constant attention, remedial actions, and recognition of growth. Still others will struggle in most areas, and they, most of all, need to have their successes illustrated to their families. Make it a practice to note the best of each child. Use that as a take-off point of discussion with parents and capitalize on those bright qualities when working on the areas of difficulty the child faces. For some, baby steps toward reaching goals are all they can muster. It is up to us to note those steps, celebrate them, and share them with their parents.

There are literally thousands of lessons and activities that teachers plan and perform throughout the school year. Documenting and celebrating the joy and success of those activities is critical. The effect of communicating these positive images is the development of a stronger relationship between home and school, one based on a more positive presentation and comprehensive knowledge of what is happening on a daily basis in their child's school life.

Connecting
Home and School

If we really believe that parents are partners in their child's education,
then we must do whatever we can to bring them into the educational
schema. One analogy we've used likens education to a pie cut into three
pieces—the parent, the school, and the student. Using this analogy, we
impress upon parents that *their* piece, because of the close connection to
the other two pieces (school and student), could spoil the whole pie. The
visual imagery of this analogy is a powerful reminder to parents of their
need to work with us and their child to maximize their child's growth.

We've explored the idea that the amount of parental involvement in
school will be dependent on a multitude of factors. It may vary according
to family desire or ability. It may also fluctuate with the number and type
of opportunities the school provides for parents. It may vary according to
the cultural or social issues the district is facing at any given time.
Regardless of the reason, it is important that the school do whatever is
needed to bridge the gap between home and school and strive to provide as
many opportunities and levels of participation as possible.

LEVELS OF PARENT PARTICIPATION

J. P. Comer describes three levels of parental participation in schools (*Educational Leadership*, March 2005). As you move from the first to the third level, the participation of the parent becomes more integral and involved. The first level involves the general support of parents in school activities and processes. The second level comprises parental involvement in daily school events. The third, and most challenging, level is one where parents are participants in school decision-making processes.

LEVEL 1: GENERAL PARENTAL SUPPORT OF SCHOOL ACTIVITIES

Level 1 typically encompasses the greatest participation of parents. This is the level in which parents provide general support to the teacher and school, and it features the usual types of school-home connections. The most common is assisting with homework and school projects. Also included in this level is parent attendance at school events such as parent-teacher conferences, open houses, Parent Teacher Organization meetings, school concerts, award ceremonies, and fundraisers. Finally, we have participation in school-home communications such as classroom and school notices and newsletters.

As technology has advanced, we now have more ways to communicate quickly and efficiently with parents. "Homework Hotlines" have been set up with phone and now Internet access. Teachers can post homework information for parents to access by phone or online. With computers, schools can now send large numbers of parents important news, event announcements, or emergency notices through e-mail blasts. Telephone trees are set up to reach parents at home or work.

In addition to the activities listed above, parents have reported that some of their favorite Level 1 activities we have used over the years include the following:

- Individual "Way to Go, Parent (or Family)" notes to moms and dads or other family members when a student does something demonstrating traits families can be proud to have encouraged (e.g., a student who gave up part of her lunch for another child who didn't like his lunch and remarked that he wished he had a lunch like hers). Sending a note to remark about their child's empathy and willingness to share reinforces the behavior and makes a positive statement about the family's worth in the child's education.

- Classroom Web sites designed and developed by the teacher and class for families to read about curriculum, grading, and upcoming events. Teachers can encourage students who do not have computers at home to visit the local library with their parents and read the Web page together as a family.
- Sending quarterly district newsletters to inform parents of districtwide events, initiatives, and issues of celebration or concern.
- Informing families of upcoming unit topics and inviting them to send in items or share stories that may be relevant to the topics.
- Sending "Good News" notes home for parents to send back their good news about their child at home.
- Setting up "Bring a Parent to School Day" so that parents can observe what happens throughout their child's school day.

LEVEL 2: PARENTAL INVOLVEMENT IN DAILY SCHOOL EVENTS

Level 2 involves bringing parents into the school on a regular basis. They may volunteer to assist in daily activities or might volunteer to help with special classroom events and projects. Typical of this level are parents who chaperone field trips or volunteer to assist with reading or math in the classroom. Some may volunteer to assist in the school library or front office weekly or monthly. Some may be involved in assisting teachers with lesson preparations or with supplemental supplies and artwork. Many parents may volunteer regularly (e.g., one or two days a week, one week per month) to work side by side with the teacher in the classroom to provide more individual assistance for students.

It is important that you solicit parent volunteers for a wide variety of valuable activities that vary in complexity and difficulty so that all parents can contribute if they wish to. On the easier-to-accommodate end, you can invite them to be receivers of information, such as coming in to be the audience for book reports or performances in the classroom. On the other end of the continuum, you can invite them to make their family interests and talents an integral part of your classroom. Let them share their culture and skills with your class. Cooking, sewing, and musical or artistic talents are just the beginning of how they can bring their fund of knowledge into the classroom.

Of course, Level 2 involvement requires more time and effort on the part of parents. Busy work schedules may hinder or prohibit volunteer time during the day. Here again, technology can be of assistance. In one of my schools, we provided a video recorder for family members to record their presentation or discussion of topics they might want to share. One Polish grandmother spent a morning in school and demonstrated how to make pierogies for one of our cooking classes doing a unit on ethnic foods. Another family videotaped their collection of antique farm machines and tools for our fourth-grade classes studying our state's farming history. Yet another mother videotaped "My Day as a Veterinarian" for our second-grade class studying community workers as part of a social studies curriculum.

When parents are involved in the school on a periodic or regular basis, all students are helped, not just the individual child of the parent who volunteers. By assisting the teacher or librarian, by helping in the lunchroom, or by working directly with the students themselves, they add a dimension that exhibits respect for families and what they bring to the school environment. They need not work only in the classroom of their child. They might work with the same grade level or a different grade level altogether. It is their assistance in the school that is important. Tapping this potential is an important way to expand what the school can offer its students, and it will go a long way toward improving the relationships between home and school.

Over the years, some of the most valuable Level 2 examples we have profited from include the following:

- Parents supporting the art teacher in the preparation and setup of art materials for specific projects
- Parents assisting in the building and painting of scenery for class or school productions
- Volunteers to read orally to students while the teacher roams the room and monitors student focus and awareness of what was being read
- Volunteer grandparents to work one-on-one with students needing help with math, reading, or spelling
- Volunteer "homework helpers" who help students who did not get their homework done at night at some point during the day
- An "office mom" who greets parents and students at the door and passes on forgotten messages or items to students

LEVEL 3: PARENTAL INVOLVEMENT IN DECISION-MAKING PROCESSES

In the third level of parent participation, parents become members of the school or district decision-making processes. Parents are represented on governance teams, hiring committees, and school-based decision-making committees. By participating in consensus-based decision-making teams, parents become an integral part of the planning process. Engaging parents in these meaningful ways (when done respectfully and in broad-based terms so as not to incur micromanagement) results in a sense of ownership for parents. These parents often become some of your best advocates.

We were employed by our district during a period when it moved from an autonomous, administrative decision-making process to a shared process that included teachers, parents, and eventually students. It was a difficult transition that took several years to assimilate into our thinking and belief systems. There were many discussions and arguments about "loss of control," who had the "final" say, and how "votes" would be taken. In the end, consensus-building teams were chosen as the best way to arrive at decisions that would be embraced by all participants.

Parents accepted positions on each of our Building Action Teams. These teams focused on myriad issues specific to their building and also worked on issues from Central Office that impacted all buildings. Together, members of the administrative and teaching staff worked with parents and sometimes students and support-staff members when appropriate. Decisions on issues such as the school's mission statement, grade-level curriculum, building renovations, teacher recruitment, and the teacher interview process were among the targeted objectives of the team.

Parents were also invited to become members of districtwide decision-making teams. One particularly successful districtwide team that bridged school and home was one I created after attending a seminar at Walt Disney World. The seminar focused on how schools could market their programs to garner support for school initiatives and practices. As participants, we learned about and witnessed the principles of meeting consumer needs that Disney follows—its goal is to have all its Disney World patrons have a good time and think Disney World is one of the best places in the world to be.

Following Disney's marketing strategies, we set out to create a committee comprised of all constituents involved in our school district. We called it the "Communicating Positive Images" committee. It was comprised of representatives from each area of our district: each school building, our district administrative office, transportation office, food service, maintenance and grounds, parents from different neighborhood schools, and business community members located within our district.

The committee's mission was developed with three goals in mind. The first goal was to identify and share with our constituents the positive happenings and initiatives throughout the district and community. The second goal was to recognize individual building or district issues and areas of concern that any school community members wanted the committee to address. The third and final goal was to brainstorm ideas on how to change negatives to positives. The committee met once a month, minutes were kept and shared throughout the district, and the superintendent was regularly included to further explore issues or ideas for resolution.

Parent input and attention to the workings and findings of the committee was positive and extremely helpful in forging strong bonds between home and school. The superintendent was meticulous at reading the minutes, talked with me frequently to get the big picture, and facilitated the resolution of any concerns or problems as quickly as possible. His attention to the workings of the committee, as well as his occasional attendance at meetings, went a long way toward building trust between the district and our families.

Level 3 activities that we have seen make a huge impact on forging bridges between home and school are the following:

- Formation of a Parent Advisory Council with parent representatives from each school meeting with the superintendent and assistant superintendent quarterly to share concerns, ask questions, and offer ideas and suggestions
- Parent membership on a districtwide building renovations committee whose goal was to inspect and survey the needs of each building, look at significant current and potential future building problems, and report findings to the superintendent
- Parent membership on Building Action Teams whose charge was to make decisions about all kinds of building issues from teacher-pupil ratios to appropriate equipment and supplies needed by staff and students
- Parent membership on District Planning Teams for various curriculum issues such as textbook adoption, dress code, and board of education policy adoption or revisions
- Parent membership on the district's Committee on Special Education
- Parent membership on administrative and staff interview teams at the building and district levels

SUMMARY

The rewards of increased parental involvement can be unprecedented for the school, parents, community, and, most importantly, the students. It is the school that must build bridges for parents to cross.

When the school is ready to set up bridges, it gains the various levels of support and assistance so vital to the foundation of positive school-home relationships. By setting up Level 1 bridges, the school gains the support of parents who simply bring an extra pair of hands on needed occasions. At Level 2, the school will benefit from parents who offer consistent and continual talents that can be easily embedded into the school routine. At a deeper level, Level 3, those parents who are willing to become part of a decision-making process can offer insights that may ultimately change the face of the school community.

Everyone reaps the rewards of strong bridges built to bring the school, parents, and community members together. Their combined efforts can only lead to the betterment of all students' growth and success. Who wouldn't want this for their school and children?

Cultivating Resources

I am only one; but still I am one. I cannot do everything, but still I can do something; I will not refuse to do the something I can do.

—Helen Keller

We've talked a lot about how we can forge strong relationships with parents. We started with a discussion of recognizing and understanding the different personalities that might be at play in our various relationships. We targeted several indicators that might signal possible roadblocks when making positive connections with home. We have identified the communication skills and basic rules needed to enhance the chance for positive relationships to form, and we offered some suggestions on ways to use creativity, flexibility, and marketing to strengthen your connection between home and school. If measured and used judiciously, these strategies will serve to gain trust and confidence in our abilities and efforts to help our students grow academically, socially, and behaviorally.

As our relationships strengthen, parents' expectations rise, and they may turn to us to help them with a multitude of personal or family problems. They often present a variety of questions and concerns regarding not only their child's academic progress but other aspects of their lives that might impact their child. The higher the respect and trust in us and what we do, the more they may come to depend on us for answers or solutions to problems they may be experiencing at home.

While many school districts across the country have begun to add community resource clinics (e.g., health clinics and family counseling centers) to their school sites, most have not. Although we work hard to help in any way that we can, we know that we cannot be the sole provider of all that our families need. Nor should we even try. However, with the variety of professionals and services in our schools, we are in the unique position of having a network of resources that allows us, at the very least, to provide families with direction toward where they might turn for support and assistance. It behooves us to take on the responsibility of collecting and providing possible resources for parents to draw on for help.

WHERE DO YOU START?

To begin with, you need to identify or analyze the most common needs of your school families. In reviewing our own families, and in discussing the needs findings of several local school communities, major commonalities emerged. The following common problem areas or concerns were noted:

- Mental health care and counseling
- Health and medical services
- Legal services
- Recreational services
- Financial services
- Employment
- Education
- Environment (e.g., water, heat, food)
- Respite (babysitting and care of disabled or aged individuals)

Once you have compiled your own list of family and community needs, you will have a foundation upon which to search and build your list of resources. These resources can then be documented, published, and disseminated to families. Some families will only need us to point them in the right direction. For others, we may need to make the connection happen. On rare occasions, for something essential to happen, we may need to be an integral part of accessing the service (e.g., going with a parent to their child's doctor's evaluation).

COMPILING A LIST OF FAMILY RESOURCES

When you look at the list of potential resources your families may need and then add the resources you and the school may need, the job of obtaining information and completing a resource list may seem daunting. Well, it is—or it *was* for someone else. Most of the time, all you will need to do is seek out what various organizations in your local or regional communities have already compiled and published. There is no need to reinvent the wheel if it already exists in one form or another and may be able to be used as is or with slight modification.

Start by making a few well-placed phone calls to local, regional, or state agencies. Ask them for copies of any manuals, handbooks, lists, or pamphlets of community services that are available and ready for use. Many organizations (e.g., emergency hotlines, Salvation Army, YMCA, childcare agencies, advocacy groups) will have already done the work for you! Their documents often contain a definition of their purpose, types of services provided, and service locations, costs, and contact numbers. The great thing about these organizations is that all you need to do is collect their publications and make them available in all of your school settings!

If you don't have time to make the phone calls yourself, ask around. Use your contacts and networks to get the information. Talk to your administration, school psychologist, social worker, special education teachers, nurses, and secretaries. All of these people have connections to different organizations and agencies and could collect information from them. Therefore, once you have made your list of desired resources, make it available to your colleagues and entire staff and ask for their help.

Some staff may volunteer with various organizations that provide services parents are looking for. Some may belong to social clubs, athletic associations, community service groups, or scouting groups—all of which serve the community and will likely be able to provide you with information on their programs and services. One source will lead to another, and before you know it, you will be on your way to compiling a detailed catalog of community supports and services that will be of unlimited value to you and your parents.

In your search, remember to use your local (city, county) and state Web sites. We have found extensive information on the Web by entering the county or state name followed by *.gov*. By accessing these government sites, you'll find many public and private agencies listed by the needs they support and how to contact them for help. You can download the information as needed and provide parents lacking Internet access with a copy.

WHAT SHOULD YOUR
RESOURCE LIST LOOK LIKE?

Once you have compiled all of your resource lists, pamphlets, and newsletters, how do you go about consolidating and disseminating them into a user-friendly package? Well, there are many different approaches. While some schools simply make the collection of published documents available in offices (e.g., main office, nurse's office, guidance office), others make the effort to repackage the information into simple packets that can be disseminated to parents.

Some schools will collect multiple sources of information and then work to compile it into a consolidated handbook for parents. Doing this results in a more user-friendly document that might list services in clusters, by type of support needed. The handbook becomes a reference for parents to use as they may need it, and it can become a very handy source of information for you as well. Most agencies are happy to help us out if we call with simple questions about their areas of expertise, and we often need to touch base with professionals to make sure we are going in the right direction at school.

You might need or want to simplify this process even more by creating a smaller pamphlet of the major sources of support available in your area. Again, it is helpful to cluster the information by type of support (e.g., legal, counseling), with the agency's name, contact number, and Web site (if available). The value of this shorter summary is that multiple copies can be handed out, and parents can take it with them for immediate use or for later reference. When a family is in need and looking for help that we may not be qualified for or capable of providing, having a portable reference tool will give them an enormous feeling of support and assist them in their search for help with their problem.

Parents inherently understand that the school district cannot be everything to every child or family. Even knowing this, it is hard for parents to accept. If you can help them to find the resources elsewhere, you will still be considered as being part of the solution. One clear example of this comes to mind. Our district ran a very large summer school program for students with disabilities. This program was forced to keep to very strict federal and state guidelines that students needed to meet in order to attend. Many times, parents of children who did not fit these guidelines would call, frustrated and angry that their children were not able to attend the program. They were, of course, disappointed that our district was not providing a summer program for all children. Explaining the legal requirements did not assuage many of them.

After a few summers of dealing with these disappointed parents, we began looking for additional options across the county available to the children we could not serve. We actually found *several*, compiled a list for our parents, and sent it home in the late spring. Parents were able to select from a variety of children's programs that served their kids academically and socially. They were happy and appreciative of our efforts. Additionally, some of these programs called us directly to thank us for "advertising" their program, which, in some cases, led to increased funding and expansion for them. All in all, taking the time to research and compile a list of summer resources was a win-win for all of us.

Once you compile this resource bank, make sure you share the wealth and make your products available to all staff. Make copies for them or leave copies in a central location (e.g., teacher's room, guidance office, teacher reference section of library). All of us have problems of one kind or another at times, and having a quick tool that can guide us to solutions is a great help. Besides, the more people who know about it, the more likely parents are to find out that the resources exist!

ONE STEP FURTHER

If you have the time or inclination, there is one more step that will benefit you and the parents you work with. Make some contacts and, where possible, forge strong connections to some of the agencies you include in your resource documents. Call or visit some of them (especially those of high priority and close proximity). Let them know who you are and why you are seeking a connection with them. Talk to them about the families you serve (without identifying information) and how they may need their help. Explain how and why you plan to distribute the information to your families. Let them know that your parents may be calling and asking for help that the school could not provide.

By establishing a direct connection and building a relationship with these agencies, you can anticipate their willingness to work with you and their understanding of why the school cannot provide the level of service the family may need. This connection may also give parents more confidence when calling the agency if they know there is a link between the school and the agency.

Another tactic is to invite agencies to your school to meet with staff and parents. Short presentations at faculty meetings are helpful to disseminate the information to all teachers quickly. It also helps the agency to understand the school community they are getting referrals from. They can give more in-depth information and discussion of their service provisions than might be in a handbook or leaflet. By making them a part of a school function, they will often become advocates for the school, rather than a separate entity that may not understand the need for parental supports outside of the schools.

Inviting various service agencies to present at parent group meetings is an excellent way to disseminate information and increase parent attendance at meetings. Themed meetings can afford multiple families an opportunity to get information and assistance in a less threatening manner than approaching an agency on their own. For many families, once they have made contact with a real person who has talked about what they do and how they approach the area of concern, taking the step to make an appointment and get direct help is much easier.

SUMMARY

We know that it is not possible for us to be the solution for all of the problems that our families face. We have a hard enough time taking care of the multitude of tasks we must manage in order to provide instruction and address the needs of the children under our care. However, we can't separate our students from their families. In July 2006, the Association for Supervision and Curriculum Development (ASCD) convened the "Commission on the Whole Child" to address the need for schools, parents, communities, and our government to work together for children. The "Whole Child" movement is about just that, recognizing and assisting our children as whole entities.

In redefining a successful learner, the ASCD recognized that children must be healthy, safe, engaged, supported, and challenged. It asks communities to look at the whole picture and make sure that each student is surrounded by qualified, caring adults. We are a primary portion of that support, and as such, must do what we can to assist in gathering others who are needed.

We must, therefore, do whatever we can to help our families deal with the issues that are preventing their children from learning and doing their best. If we can't help directly, then we need to do what we can to direct them to the sources that *can* help them. By doing so, we help our students. By helping our students, we enhance their ability to learn. It's really as simple as that. Build the relationships with your families, cultivate the resources they may need, make the connections with those resources, and support your families as best you can.

Summarizing Global Lessons Learned

View life as a continuous learning experience.

—Denis Waitley, author, speaker,
and productivity consultant

Our successes and mistakes, upon analysis and reflection, have imparted several essential principles to abide by in our quest to forge positive relationships between home and school. When these basic principles are followed, the outcomes we experience usually turn out favorably. When we have deviated from these principles, the outcomes usually resulted in problems between home and school. That's not to say that if followed, outcomes will always be positive, just that a positive result will be more likely. As we look at these principles, we will be revisiting several ideas we have considered previously. We offer this final chapter as a summary of the essentials to building strong parent-school relationships.

LESSON 1: KEEP THE STUDENT FRONT AND CENTER

Our work as educators is all about the student and what he or she needs to learn and grow as a whole individual. Our efforts are on behalf of our students, and we must keep this essential premise front and center in all that we do in our role as educators. It is a given that we will encounter myriad problems and frustrations along the way, but we need to deal with the problems and issues surrounding each child without ever losing sight of the individual we are charged to educate.

Having said all that, the learning, social, behavioral, interpersonal, and family issues students bring with them can be daunting. They can overwhelm our best intentions and thwart our best efforts to help them make progress. But we can't give up. Educators have hard work in front of them under the best of circumstances. When encountering any obstacles, we must remind ourselves that it's all about our students and our efforts to help them maximize their potential.

What we have learned, time after time, from some of our most difficult parental situations is that they, too, want their children to succeed. It might not always be evident, or maybe it's *too* evident, that they are beating you up with their own frustrations. But they generally want the same thing: for their child to do well. When asked outright, parents repeat variations of the same desired outcomes from sending their child to school: academic success, learned social and interpersonal skills, and appropriate behavior.

If you adhere to this first rule, focusing your efforts with the best interests of the student front and center, parents realize that you are, ultimately, on their side. They can see that you are focused on their child, and it's not about you against them or you against the child. It will go a long way toward building trust in your motives and actions, and it will help peel away doubts and fears that their child's best interests are not center stage.

I recall one particularly difficult grandmother and guardian who came to our team meeting to discuss some behavioral issues that had arisen with her grandson. She entered the room, pushed her chair back from the table, folded her arms across her body, and glared at us. It felt a little like she was daring us to provoke her into saying something harsh. We began with an overall assessment of her grandson. We talked about his positive qualities, his academic bright spots, his interpersonal charm, and why we thought he had great potential. Then we slowly wove a description of what he was doing to thwart his progress and interrupt his learning. Finally, we asked her if she had any insights on how we could "help him to alter his behavior to enhance his learning, instead of sabotaging it." Then we waited and kept quiet. A full two minutes passed. Finally, she uncrossed her arms, looked us in the eye, and said, "Well, it's about time that I met a bunch of teachers who aren't just waiting on their paychecks!" We all laughed and then entered into a good discussion of strategies we could use at school and home to help this young man. The strategies worked. She was on our side, her grandson knew that we were working together, and his behavior improved dramatically with some direct talking between home and school.

On another occasion, we were working with a mother who wanted a specialized service for her daughter. The service would require additional time out of the classroom and, in our opinion, was a duplication of a service already provided. Additionally, we felt strongly that taking the student out of her primary classroom and missing the instruction that occurred while she was gone would serve only to undermine her learning. After several minutes of discussion and pleading with the mother to at least let us set a trial period, she agreed to hold off on the outside service because she knew that the school "always puts my daughter's interests and needs front and center."

Keep the student front and center in all discussions, keeping the focus on his or her abilities and needs. In doing so, you create an environment that demonstrates your commitment to serving the student to the best of your ability and with utmost priority. With a few possible exceptions now and then, parents will appreciate and value you more if they know that their child's needs come first.

LESSON 2: BE THE BEST COMMUNICATOR YOU CAN BE

Communication is the key to establishing and maintaining positive relationships with parents. It involves the transfer of information between schools and home in such a way that trust and confidence are built with each interaction. It requires both senders and receivers to be good listeners, observers, and relaters of the messages being conveyed.

The burden of the communication processes between home and school lies on us. We must become the best listeners we can be. We must "listen" with our ears, eyes, and minds. We need to be cautious and think through our messages before sending them—especially when the message is less than positive. We need to pay attention to the verbal and nonverbal statements and gestures we use that can either enhance what we are trying to convey or break down the communication completely. One thing is sure: teachers and schools who communicate well build more positive bonds between home and school. Those that don't work at good communication skills have major problems with their parental relationships.

I've worked with several districts that were experiencing major problems with lack of parental involvement or the development of highly negative relationships between home and school. In each case, analyzing the communication systems in place, improving the amount and nature of parental contacts, and focusing on improving the verbal and nonverbal skills of staff helped facilitate the development of more frequent and positive relationships between home and school.

Communicating with non-English-speaking parents can be particularly difficult. We must pay attention to these parents and make sure we find a way to communicate with them directly. While students may carry information home to their parents, we cannot rely on its accuracy or be certain that the message will be conveyed.

It is critical that districts locate and use interpreters within or outside their schools to assist with communications to and from culturally diverse families and non-English-speaking parents. Technology can certainly help us translate words from one language to another, but finding and using interpreters who can facilitate a meeting or translate a newsletter to parents in their native language is invaluable. Nothing says "we care enough to go the extra mile to make sure we can share information together" better than the hiring or finding of a live person who can make communication easier and more accurate.

One school district, with a particularly heavy influx of non-English-speaking Hispanic families, made a point of finding or hiring individuals at each location who could speak directly with, or interpret for, families when home and school needed to communicate directly. They then established an English class for these families and provided babysitters during the class for siblings who were not in school. Additionally, they hired a Hispanic individual from the community to translate all of their important communiqués into Spanish before they were sent home. The end result was increased appreciation for the district and parental involvement in school. A college or university in your area can be a rich resource for interpreters, especially those of more obscure dialects.

Whatever the communication difficulties, it is imperative that you search for ways to improve parents' ease and comfort when they are interacting with you. The more consistent and positive your communications are, the more parents will come to rely on them, desire them, and feel more at ease with making and maintaining contact with you. Improved communication translates to improved relationships.

LESSON 3: BECOME USER-FRIENDLY

Nothing speaks to being user-friendly as much as a school climate that is inviting and responsive to its participants. Take a good look at your classrooms and school. How does it present itself visually? What processes or rules govern parent participation—their ability to come in and visit, volunteer, or meet with staff? Ask yourself if the ambiance of your setting is warm and friendly or if parents find it closed and unwelcoming.

Your school and classrooms need to be easy to navigate. Parents must be made aware of how and when they are able to confidently reach the people they need (e.g., teachers, school nurse, principal, guidance counselor). The people who greet them when they call or come to the school, the "first responders," so to speak, must be welcoming and friendly. These responders must be able to answer frequently asked questions, supply general information about schedules and events, direct calls quickly and efficiently to appropriate personnel if necessary, and, above all, take accurate and thorough messages when needed.

If a school and its teachers are seen as responsive, the overall perception of the school climate is one that is user-friendly. Of course, guidelines need to be established so that interruptions are not too frequent or so random that they disrupt the educational process. We've found that once parents know the guidelines and *why* they are in place, they do not mind and, in most cases, respect and support them.

Take some time to provide discussion and training for office secretaries and teaching and administrative staff on appropriate attitude, responses, and note taking when interacting with families and the community. We have all encountered friendly secretaries who seem to go out of their way to assist you when you've called the school. They might take the time to look up an answer to your question or call you back when they found an answer. They might have transferred your call to a real person who has the answer. They might have carefully taken down your question and later returned your call or had someone else with the answer call you. Perhaps they might have simply assured you that your message will get to the appropriate person.

Contrast those responses with the response of a secretary who says hello, quickly says "I'll transfer your call," and never attempts to ask for information, offers any assurances, or provides a response of any kind. What about the secretary who seems to be put out that you called? Or, think about the secretary who gives you the bum's rush with a "sorry, the principal is not in" and hangs up before you can even ask your question!

Schools need a climate that screams "come on in!" There needs to be a location for parents to sit and review books, records, newsletters, and anything else that they might need or want to read before meeting with a teacher or administrator. Most schools have one or two chairs in the main office entryway. Usually, district newsletters, calendars, educational pamphlets, and even local newspapers are located on a table next to the chairs. This is where they are asked to wait until they can meet with the person(s) they came to talk with.

We submit that parents need more than that to truly feel like their participation in the school is welcomed. They need a location that lets them know that it is expected that parents will be at school for various reasons and that their time there is important and has been given priority by the specific allocation of space to meet their needs.

Some of the best examples of "parent areas" that we've seen involve the actual allocation of space for a parent area in the building. Space in most schools is tight. But if we are to convince parents that we really want them to be a partner in the education of their children, we *must* give them their own area in which to come, talk with other parents, find helpful resources to assist them in helping their children learn, and meet together to discuss common issues.

Some schools are fortunate enough to have a full room to allocate as a parent conference room or parent library. However, many schools are crowded, and space is limited even for the educational programs it must provide. In one overcrowded middle school building, in which there was not a single room that could be allocated, the principal got very creative. She allocated an area in one of her entrance lobbies (about 12×20 feet) and had district maintenance personnel construct temporary walls to make a "room" for parents to use. This area held a conference table with six chairs and two bookcases of pamphlets, newsletters, articles, books, and videos as part of a lending library for parents to use. It took a while for parents to learn about it and try it out, but it now is one of the central places for parents to visit and is used almost daily. Of course, all fire codes were adhered to, and materials in this space followed privacy rules (i.e., no records or videos of actual children in the school were stored there).

A clean and tidy area that displays student work, school events, awards, and themes is key to a user-friendly climate. Parents reported that they felt most closely tied to those schools (and classrooms) that clearly displayed what was happening in their child's school day. They loved being provided with their child's daily schedule, maps of the school so that they could see where and how their child moved about, and newsletters and calendars alerting them to upcoming events and results of their child's activities and events. In short, parents need and want to know what is going on at all times. Even the most seemingly disenfranchised parents reported that they appreciated the school's efforts to be open and welcoming to them when and if they could be involved.

Other good ways to be user-friendly include the following:

- Provision of greeters at front door
- Placement of clear signage in entrance and along hallways to direct parents to specific locations throughout the building

- Creation of a "job description" book for volunteers explaining the many ways that parents can volunteer their time in the building
- Development of newsletters that are quick and easy to read with consistent columns for important topics and calendar events
- Color-coding school communications so parents know, for example, that all yellow communications come from the school nurse, all blue come from the principal's office, or all green come from the classroom
- Provision of adult chairs in the classroom for parents
- Scheduling of regular parent-invited events above and beyond the typical holiday events (e.g., a 15-minute morning meeting held every day to review announcements, give awards, or note special achievements)

LESSON 4: BE PROACTIVE

There are two procedural methods to choose between when dealing with parents and trying to forge partnerships between school and home. You can choose to be proactive in your strategies or you can decide to be reactive and wait to respond to parents' actions (or nonactions) with your efforts to involve them. Obviously, this entire book has demonstrated that we believe the proactive approach is a far more effective and rewarding method of developing and forging positive relationships with parents. It is interesting to note that the thesaurus cites *practical*, *positive*, and *upbeat* as synonyms for *proactive* and *hasty*, *imprudent*, and *rash* as synonyms for *reactive*!

Teachers lead very busy lives. There is so much to do in a day that we are often left with things that we can't get to by the end of the day, week, or even month. It is human nature to procrastinate on the things that might not be right in front of us or, in particular, might be more difficult or uncomfortable to deal with. However, when you choose a wait-and-see approach, one that forces you to react to what didn't go away or finally happened, you leave yourself open to myriad events that, once allowed to occur, may be much more difficult to handle. The old adage about sweeping things under the rug is true. By the time you get around to taking care of the huge pile in your way, the time spent, the energy expended, and the feelings developed may be totally counter to your original intent.

On the other hand, by adopting proactive strategies in your attempts to build positive relationships with parents, you may actually *prevent* many problems that might arise. If you think ahead and act proactively, you might attenuate problems that arise and might be the first to deal with issues you think might become problematic if practical actions are not taken.

One particularly clear example of the virtue of being proactive comes, to my chagrin, from a situation in which I did not go far enough to be proactive. One year we had a particularly unruly group of fourth graders who constantly landed in my office (principal) with extremely inappropriate behaviors toward one another and other members of the school community. The behaviors were hurtful and sometimes dangerous (e.g., bullying, fighting). The percentage of students involved in this group was high (approximately 75 percent). I worked proactively, or so I thought, and consistently talked to them individually and in groups. I told them that if these behaviors continued, the grade level would not be given the privilege of their annual class trip. To make a long story short, the students did not demonstrate improved behavior to the point where I could be comfortable allowing them to go off on a long class trip representing the school. Needless to say, when the annual class trip was canceled, the uproar from the kids was great, but the anger and outrage of their parents was even more pronounced. While the trip remained canceled, I ended up having multiple meetings explaining why the trip was canceled and had very negative feelings from many of those parents for years to come.

In retrospect, I should have involved the parents of this grade level in a general-information meeting early on. I should have explained what was happening in specific, objective, factual terms (i.e., provided the parents with specific behaviors, frequency of behaviors, percentage of students involved, impact of the behaviors). I should have asked for their suggestions and support in turning the behaviors around and in getting consensus on what the outcome should be if the behaviors did not improve. I'm convinced that with their involvement in the solution, I would have either had a better outcome or more support and less anger when and if the trip was canceled.

In another instance, involving a young man, one teacher took a proactive approach with a family who was always a "no show" for conferences, events, and telephone calls. The teacher, in talking with the boy, discovered that it was his grandmother who he seemed to like and care about most. She called the grandmother, who said, "No one ever called me before, and I'm the one who really watches him and takes care of him." She came into school for a conference, met with all of the boy's teachers, set up a regular communication system with the classroom teacher, and visibly supported the school efforts at home. Things dramatically improved with the boy's behavior, and he showed academic improvement as well.

The aim of being proactive is to position yourself in such a manner that you think positively, condition yourself to weigh your words and actions carefully, and prepare yourself to put your best foot forward in dealing with students and families. If parents feel that you are trying your best and putting effort into avoiding problems, if they know that you are including them in the educational process, and you are demonstrating to them that you honestly care about their child, your work will be easier and your relationships with parents will more likely be positive. Make sure that you are visible, accessible, and involved *before* a problem occurs.

LESSON 5: VIEW PARENTS AND FAMILIES AS OPPORTUNITIES TO BRING DIVERSITY, INTERESTS, AND TALENTS INTO THE CLASSROOM AND SCHOOL

If we are to build strong relationships between home and school, then we must respect the differences in cultures, talents, skills, interests, and experiences our children bring with them to school. Every family has something to share that can afford us the opportunity to learn more about each other, allow us to know more about the professions and backgrounds of our families, and enable us to design lessons that bring a greater knowledge base to our students.

Our communities are becoming more culturally diverse. We now have better, more direct chances to expose our students to the different nationalities and cultures of the world we live in. We need to capitalize on these opportunities and work specifically to bring more diversity to our teaching. Food, language, history, homelands, and special talents and occupations are just a sampling of the types of areas that we can build our discussions and demonstrations around. What better way for our families to invest in our educational process than giving them some ownership through sharing their personal cultures and experiences with us in a meaningful way?

One middle school I visited set up a "parent volunteer" blackboard in each classroom on the night of their open house. On the board were columns of suggested volunteer activities for parents, with another column for them to write their own suggestions. One open column was titled "I am willing to _____," with a place for a signature next to the open line. Teachers told me they were often surprised at what turned out to be wonderful parental ideas. For example, one father wrote, "Demonstrate to the students how to change the oil in their car." Another mother wrote, "Write out (scribe) what any student with writing difficulties wants to write as they dictate it." Yet another parent wrote, "Teach a group lesson on butterflies (her hobby) while the teacher works with students one on one who need help with something."

If parents are made to feel that their lives and work are interesting and valuable to the school, they will be more willing to share their ideas and participate in school activities. More importantly, if the school can give parents who don't feel they have anything to offer an opportunity to be involved and appreciated for who they are or what they know or do, you have a bond that will be hard to break. Such was the case of a grandmother who spoke little English but was an expert at making painted eggs for Ukrainian Easter. She was asked to come in and demonstrate her talent for a class activity on different holiday customs.

One school in the Adirondack Mountains of New York worked to get at least one parent of each child involved in a minimum of one activity during the school year. Many of the families were very poor and led time-consuming, difficult lives logging and mining. The school created a "work week" in which different types of work were honored and parents came in to discuss all kinds of jobs. Professionals talked about being doctors and lawyers, loggers explained the logging business, miners talked about the type of mining they did, and hotel workers talked about the various jobs at the hotels that surrounded the local lake. At the end of the week, a book was put together that celebrated the myriad jobs that made up the fabric of the district lives. Each job was respected, all were acknowledged, and the benefits of the diverse community activities were honored. More importantly, strong relationships were born from that initiative, and community pride in the school district increased.

If you give your parents the curriculum topics and a road map of when and how you will navigate through the areas of study, you will be more likely to have them invest in their child's education. Ask them to explore ways that they can be a partner in exploring the curriculum with you. The collective experiences, wealth of knowledge, and myriad skills your many families will bring with their diverse lives can serve only to expand and improve your teaching throughout the year. These multiple talents, skills, and life experiences will build a stronger foundation for your relationships to rest on.

LESSON 6: ABOVE ALL, KEEP AND USE A SENSE OF HUMOR

There is no better way to establish and maintain a positive relationship than by employing a sense of humor. Humor is one of the most effective tools you can use to demonstrate your pleasure, passion, and joy with your profession and the students you teach. Because laughter and humor are contagious, it will be difficult to remain negative once exposed.

A mentor and supervising professor of student teachers once told us that "teaching is either the easiest or the hardest job in the world, depending on how seriously you take it." She was right. To do a good job, to make a difference in the lives of the students under our charge, and to ensure the best possible academic, social, and behavioral outcomes for each student is downright difficult. It not only costs us professionally, it costs us personally.

In education, we see a picture of our entire society. We see its riches and its trials and tribulations. While there is much to be celebratory about, there are also sad circumstances in our students' lives. We need to find the joy and uplifting parts of each child's story and focus on those while, at the same time, using humor to fight the negative.

Mel Brooks said, "Humor is just another defense against the universe." Bill Cosby states, "You can turn a painful situation around through laughter. If you can find humor in anything, even poverty, you can survive it." That's what we must do. Laugh often and loudly. Look for the humor around you in the situations you face. Cultivate an atmosphere of humor in your parental relationships. They will become stronger for it.

In the end, we realize that we are all in this thing we call *education* together: teachers, administrators, students, parents, and community. There are going to be conflicts. Use humor to attenuate the negative feelings. A well-placed laugh signals that you are enjoying the relationship and are gaining some benefit from it.

Humor carries some risk with it. You must be careful not to make jokes or poke fun at anyone, so be sure that the humor is not personal. Start by greeting your parents with a smile. It tells them that you are happy to see them and value their participation in whatever the event is, whether a face-to-face parent conference or a large school event.

It might take some time to use humor with some parents or to find the humor in some situations. We worked with a colleague who was a master at summarizing the most difficult situations with a single, hysterically funny closing sentence that very often diffused the negative emotions flowing through a meeting. After one particularly lengthy parent conference in which almost all of us had shed some tears about what had happened to the family and child, this colleague stood up, reached for a box of facial tissues, and sternly announced, "OK, drinks at my place. All of you are invited; follow me!" She then proceeded to her classroom and set up a conference table with juice, cookies, and candy she had left over from a party that day. The amazing thing was that the parents followed, and we all laughed and joked about other nonpersonal things for a half hour before they left for home.

Enjoy what you do. Find the enjoyment, search for the half-full part of each glass, and spread the humor. Smile, laugh, joke, be playful, and entertain your parents, despite the circumstances that might surround you both. Be especially vigilant to use humor with those who tend to see the half-empty part of each glass. After all, we're all in this together.

SUMMARY

We need to take the time to analyze and reflect on how our attitudes, practices, and behaviors affect our relationships. Doing so will allow us to recognize specific patterns or actions that have influenced the development of those relationships. Examining these patterns will then permit us to differentiate the universal lessons that can be learned from both positive and negative experiences.

This chapter has provided the reader with six general tenets that have been proven to facilitate the development of strong, positive relationships between teachers, administrators, and parents. Employing these tenets will provide a platform for supporting the desired connections between school and home.

Resource A

Discover Your Personality

In each box, choose the words that best describe your personality. Double the number of words you chose in each box and record that number.

LION		OTTER	
Likes authority	Takes charge	Enthusiastic	Takes risks
Confident	Determined	Visionary	Motivates
Firm	Enterprising	Energetic	Very verbal
Enjoys challenges	Competitive	Promoter	Friendly
Problem solver	Productive	Mixes easily	Enjoys popularity
Bold	Purposeful	Fun-loving	Likes variety
Goal-driven	Adventurous	Spontaneous	Enjoys change
Strong-willed	Independent	Creative new ideas	Group oriented
Self-reliant	Controlling	Optimistic	Initiates
Persistent	Action-oriented	Infectious laughter	Inspirational
"Let's do it now!"		"Trust me! It'll work out!"	
Double the number chosen: _____		Double the number chosen: _____	
GOLDEN RETRIEVER		**BEAVER**	
Dependable	Good listening	Enjoys instructions	Accurate
Calm	skills	Consistent	Controlled
Not demanding	Loyal	Reserved	Predictable
Avoids	Even-keeled	Practical	Orderly
confrontations	Gives in	Factual	Conscientious
Enjoys routine	Indecisive	Perfectionist	Discerning
Warm and	Dislikes change	Detailed	Analytical
relational	Dry humor	Inquisitive	Precise
Adaptable	Sympathetic	Persistent	Scheduled
Thoughtful	Nurturing	Sensitive	Deliberate
Patient	Tolerant		
	Peacemaking	"How was it done in the past?"	
"Let's keep things the way they are."			
Double the number chosen: _____		Double the number chosen: _____	

Source: Dr. Gary Smalley and Dr. John Trent, Smalley Relationship Center (www.smalleyonline.com).

Resource B

The Animal Test

Directions: Read each statement carefully. Place a *4* to the left of the description that best characterizes you, a *3* to the left of the description that next best describes you, a *2* to the left of the description that next best describes you, and a *1* to the left of the description that least describes you. Use each number only once. No ties!

1. When pressured I . . .

    ____take charge ____get motivated ____defer to others ____wait or quit

2. I'm the kind of person who is . . .

    ____competitive ____creative ____friendly ____perfectionist

3. The word that best describes me is . . .

    ____controlling ____optimistic ____sensitive ____consistent

4. I usually . . .

    ____reach my goals ____like variety ____dislike change ____am detailed

5. The phrase that best describes me is that I . . .

    ____have a few good friends ____am popular ____have warm friendships ____am a loner

6. The phrase that best describes me is that I am . . .

    ____always busy ____fun-loving ____nurturing ____orderly

TOTALS: _____ _____ _____ _____

___

Source: Adapted from Dr. Gary Smalley and Dr. John Trent, Smalley Relationship Center (www.smalleyonline.com).

Resource C

Personality Types

Smalley and Trent have determined that there are four types of "work animals," or personality types. These four types are *lion, otter, golden retriever*, and *beaver*. Essentially, the traits of each are as follows:

LION: This personality likes to lead. Lions are good at making decisions and are very goal-oriented. They like challenges, difficult assignments, and opportunities for advancement. Lions dominate and can be aggressive and competitive. They are strong-willed, action-oriented, and always busy. Lions are the people in an organization who can usually be heard saying "Let's do it now." Areas of weakness can be their argumentative nature and a tendency to be too dictatorial. Understand that Lions *need* to roar. Under pressure, they will attack. They can be insensitive to the needs of others and opinionated or unsympathetic. Lions are the productive, determined, adventurous members of the group. Lions are most useful in leadership positions.

OTTER: Otters are very social creatures. They enjoy influencing and motivating others. They are the "idea people" in the organization. They are creative, flexible, and humorous. These folks like to hurry and finish jobs. They usually have lots of friends but not deep relationships. They are optimistic and, under pressure, will attack the task at hand. Usually, their space is messy as they can be disorganized. These people are verbal. They will ask, "How was it done in the past?" and then improve on it. They do not mind following directions and are the ones who will say, "Trust me—I'll work it out," and they do. These are the visionaries, energizers, enthusiasts, and cheerleaders in the group. Otters make great second lieutenants or leaders of a delegated task.

GOLDEN RETRIEVER: Golden retrievers are gentle personalities that love people. They are calm, good-natured, and dependable. They develop deep relationships. They are very loyal and not demanding. They seek security and do not like change. They can be very sensitive and can be easily hurt. They look for appreciation and will avoid conflict if at all possible. Under pressure, they will give in and can be easily taken advantage of. They enjoy routine and are the people who will say, "Let's keep things the way they are." They are the peacemakers, the nurturers, the thoughtful and patient members of the group. Golden retrievers make great soldiers focused on getting the job done.

BEAVER: Beavers are highly organized. They are sensitive, predictable, and orderly. They think there is a right way to do everything and want to do it exactly that way. They are perfectionists. They desire to solve things. Everything has its place, and everything goes in its place. They need more time to complete work. You cannot hurry a beaver. They prefer a slower pace. They do not like sudden changes. These are the people who you might hear saying, "Let's think on it for a while" or "How was it done in the past?" They are not very flexible, but they can be very creative. These are the analytical, detailed, and practical members of the group who take their time and do it right.

Source: Dr. Gary Smalley and Dr. John Trent, Smalley Relationship Center (www.smalley online.com).

References and Recommended Readings

Allen, J. (2008). Family partnerships that count. *Educational Leadership, 66*(1), 22–27.

Berkowitz, M., & Bier, M. (2005). Character education: Parents as partners. *Educational Leadership, 63*(1), 64–69.

Blanchard, K. (2002). *Whale done: The power of positive relationships.* New York: The Free Press.

Blank, M., & Berg, A. (2006). *All together now: Sharing responsibility for the whole child.* A report for the Commission on the Whole Child convened by the Association for Supervision and Curriculum Development. Alexandria, VA. Available online at www.ascd.org/ASCD/pdf/sharingresponsibility.pdf

Brown, E. B. (1999). *Living successfully with screwed-up people.* Grand Rapids, MI: Fleming H. Revell.

Canter, L., & Canter, M. (2001). *Parents on your side: A guide to creating positive relationships with parents* (2nd ed.). Los Angeles: Canter & Associates.

Comer, J. (2005). The rewards of parent participation. *Educational Leadership, 62*(6), 38–42.

Davis, C., & Yang, A. (2005). *Parents and teachers working together.* Turners Falls, MA: Northeast Foundation for Children.

Epstein, J. L., and Associates. (2009). *School, family, and community partnerships: Your handbook for action.* Thousand Oaks, CA: Corwin.

Forni, P. M. (2002). *Choosing civility: The twenty-five rules of considerate conduct.* New York: St. Martin's Press.

Freemantle, D. (2004). *The buzz: Fifty little things that make a big difference to world class customer service.* Boston: Nicholas Brealey Publishing.

Glasgow, N. A., & Hicks, C. D. (2003). *What successful teachers do: Research-based classroom strategies for new and veteran teachers.* Thousand Oaks, CA: Corwin.

Heller, R. (1999). *Dealing with people.* New York: DK Publishing, Inc.

Henderson, A. T., & Berla, N. (Eds.). (1994). *A new generation of evidence: The family is critical to student achievement.* Columbia, MD: National Committee for Citizens in Education.

Henderson, A. T., & Mapp, K. (2002). *A new wave of evidence: The impact of school, family and community connections on student achievement.* Austin, TX: National Center for Family and Community Connections with Schools, Southwest Educational Development Lab.

Kimball, K., Jr. (1996). *Educational excellence for your child: A how-to guide to increase the possibility your child will receive an excellent elementary, middle or high school education.* Wellfleet, MA: Leesome Associates.

Magee, M. (1995). *The principles of positive leadership: Lessons for positive living.* Philadelphia: Spencer Books.

Marzano, R. J. (2003). *What works in schools: Translating research into action.* Alexandria, VA: Association for Supervision and Curriculum Development (ASCD).

Matuszny, R., Banda, D., & Coleman, T. (2007). A progressive plan for building collaborative relationships with parents from diverse backgrounds. *Teaching Exceptional Children, 39*(4), 24–31.

On Purpose Associates. (2008). *Right brain vs. left brain.* Retrieved from http://www.funderstanding.com/right_left_brain.cfm

Ornstein, R. E. (1997). *The right mind: Making sense of the hemispheres.* San Francisco: Harcourt Brace.

Ornstein, R. E., & Thompson, R. F. (1984). *The amazing brain.* Boston: Houghton Mifflin.

Pink, D. H. (2006). *A whole new mind: Why right-brainers will rule the future.* New York: Riverhead Books.

Poverty and education: Children and adolescents. (2002). In *Education Encyclopedia.* Farmington Hills, MI: The Gale Group.

Quenk, N. L. (2000). *Essentials of Myers-Briggs type indicator assessment (essentials of psychological assessment).* New York: John Wiley & Sons.

Rath, T., & Clifton, D. O. (2004). *How full is your bucket?* New York: Gallup Press.

Rothstein-Fisch, C., & Trumbull, E. (2008). *Managing diverse classrooms: How to build on students' cultural strengths.* Alexandria, VA: Association for Supervision and Curriculum Development (ASCD).

Ruiz, D. M. (1997). *The four agreements.* San Rafael, CA: Amber-Allen Publishing.

SARK. (1994). *Living juicy: Daily morsels for your creative soul.* Berkeley, CA: Celestial Arts.

Schwarzrock, S., & Wrenn, C. G. (1973). *You always communicate something.* Circle Pines, MN: American Guidance Service.

Stone, R. (2004). *Best teaching practices for reaching all learners: What award-winning classroom teachers do.* Thousand Oaks, CA: Corwin.

Stuart, S., Flis, L., & Rinaldi, C. (2006). Connecting with families. *Teaching Exceptional Children, 39*(1), 46–51.

Trent, J., Trent, C., Smalley, G., & Smalley, N. (1992). *The treasure tree.* Dallas, TX: Word Publishing.

U.S. Census Bureau. (2007). http://www.census.gov/econ/census07

Villegas, A., & Lucas, T. (2007). The culturally responsive teacher. *Educational Leadership, 64*(6), 28–33.

Whitaker, T., & Fiore, D. J. (2001). *Dealing with difficult parents: And with parents in difficult situations.* Larchmont, NY: Eye on Education.

Index

CORWIN
A SAGE Company

The Corwin logo—a raven striding across an open book—represents the union of courage and learning. Corwin is committed to improving education for all learners by publishing books and other professional development resources for those serving the field of PreK–12 education. By providing practical, hands-on materials, Corwin continues to carry out the promise of its motto: **"Helping Educators Do Their Work Better."**